INTELLECTUAL FOUNDATIONS
FOR
INFORMATION PROFESSIONALS

Edited by Herbert K. Achleitner

SOCIAL SCIENCE MONOGRAPHS, BOULDER
DISTRIBUTED BY COLUMBIA UNIVERSITY PRESS, NEW YORK

1987

TABLE OF CONTENTS

PART IV
DISCUSSION OF PAPERS

PREFACE

The School of Library and Information Management at Emporia State University organized, with the cooperation of the Information Institute, International Academy at Santa Barbara, a three day conference in November 1984. The purpose was to provide a forum for discussion of vital issues affecting the discipline of information science and the education of information professionals.

While the concept of information science as a unified discipline is being debated, and agreement concerning its intellectual foundations is still emerging, I think that the fields represented at this conference—librarianship, management information systems, information resource management—are having an impact on research, education, and practice.

I am proud that we were able to organize and host the conference and I am pleased to have had such a distinguished group of librarians, information scientists and information professionals committed to exploring and clarifying the relationship among the information professions.

I wish to acknowledge and thank the conference chair, Herbert Achleitner, and Eric Boehm, Chairman of the International Academy at Santa Barbara. Together these two gentlemen were responsible for the selection of presenters, rapporteurs, and commentators. The School of Library and Information Management faculty members Barbara Herrin, Joni Bodart, Brian O'Connor, Marylouise Meder, Florence DeHart and Ron Haselhuhn, as well as the School's students were instrumental in the smooth functioning of conference activities. I wish to thank all participants for having made this a dynamic conference.

Robert Grover, Dean
School of Library and
Information Management

FORWARD

"Intellectual Foundations for Information Professions: Criteria for New Educational Programs" was the theme of a three day conference 16-18 November 1984. Our intention was to continue the work begun by the Information Institute of the International Academy of Santa Barbara at their conference on "Education for Information Management" in 1982. This volume includes a series of papers delivered at the Emporia conference as well as the record of discussions, working sessions and plenary sessions.

In commissioning the papers two themes were suggested: first, to examine the three streams of education for information professionals; and second, to determine if intellectual foundations can be identified that can lead to an integrated educational program. In addition the contributors were asked to explore commonalities and differences in the three educational and conceptual streams; to describe skills and values common to the three streams; and to explore the relationship between theory base and professional core practice within each of the identified streams.

The authors, presenting a cross-section of current thinking on the theoretical basis of information science, represent diverse backgrounds including information science and library science (Library/Information Science Schools), information systems (MIS) and information resources management (Records/Archives).

To the organizers it was obvious that information transfer needed a conceptual framework for its theory and research just as other disciplines do. It was hoped that by bringing together the three types of existing information streams and by exploring "commonalities and differences," we could overcome some of the differences inherent in fields with different academic traditions and move towards some sort of cross-disciplinary mode of access to the entire spectrum of scholarship.

The papers received were clustered into three sessions, with the first session proposing concepts and foundations for an information science discipline. The second session focused on applications, suggesting educational models for information resources management, including archives and records management. Information science as an academic discipline was the topic of the last session. Each session was followed by commentator's analysis and by a general discussion.

Session three was followed by three group working-sessions. Each group was given a general topic and related questions.

Group A: Commonalities and differences of the three educational and conceptual streams.

What is the relationship between theory base and professional core practice within each of the identified streams?

What are the values and skills common to the three streams?

Group B: The relationship between an academic discipline and professional practice.

What are the integrated M.A. and Ph.D. curricula for information professionals.

What are the elements of an undergraduate program for information science?

What is the status of an interdisciplinary approach at your university campus?

Group C: What are the implications for the public/private sector?

What is theplace for a Chief Information Officer in a large enterprise?

What would be an integrated executive program for Chief Executive Officer's?

At the final group working-session, rapporteurs and chairpersons reported their findings to the conference participants. The discussion centered on recommendations for educational programs and appropriate follow-up to the Santa Barbara and Emporia conferences.

The purpose of this volume then is primarily to share the ideas presented in the papers and the subsequent ideas that these generated. It is our hope that these ideas will contribute to the intellectual integration of the three streams.

My principal debt as editor of this book is to Roger Greer. It was with Dean Greer, who provided useful criticism in developing the topic, theme, and purpose, that I originally discussed the idea of organizing this conference. I am also very grateful to Eric Boehm, Chairman of the International Academy, for suggesting speakers and helping to plan the conference.

I would like to express my appreciation to the authors who gave thought and time to the topic and made the conference a reality. I wish to thank the commentators, W. Stanley Brown, Elizabeth Eddison, Fenwich Holmes, Philip James, Donald Marchand, Florence Mason, and Jane Robbins-Carter who carefully read the papers, sparked discussions, and helped make the forums productive. In particular, I want to record my thanks to the rapporteurs, Martha Hale, Ben Franckowiak, and Allen Veaner, who painstakingly took notes during the discussions. Both groups spent additional time helping me sift and synthesize a mountain of notes. My special thanks to Martha Hale for contributing valuable criticism and co-authoring the concluding chapter.

Finally, I have received widespread support from Emporia State University for this project. Dean Robert Grover and my colleagues, Joni Bodart, Florence DeHart, Nancy Flott, Ron Haselhuhn, Barbara Herrin, Marylouise Meder, Henry Stewart, Sue Hatfield, Nan Martin, and Barb Robins provided continual help. I take pleasure in acknowledging the assistance of the School's students, especially Ellen Searle and Maurice Tsai. And a special thanks is due to our secretary, Anita Woods. Emporia State University and the School of Library and Information Management provided all financial support. To all my deepest thanks and gratitude.

Eric H. Boehm

INTRODUCTION

THE COMMITMENT TO EDUCATION BY THE INTERNATIONAL ACADEMY'S INFORMATION INSTITUTE

This conference is attended by three of the four principal professionals of the Information Institute of the International Academy, and twelve of its Advisory Board serve here as speakers, rapporteurs, and commentators.

Why has the Information Institute of the International Academy at Santa Barbara gladly acceded to Emporia's request to be a co-sponsor? I welcome the opportunity to tell a bit about our past and to explain the present posture of the Information Institute. In the process I want briefly to refer to the resources we bring to bear on the issues at hand.

The Academy is a 24-year-old institution of which the Information Institute is a part. The Academy publishes three information services that appear in serial form. Our publishing activity gives us the benefit of being practitioners as well as visionaries for the Information Age. As visionaries, an information flow study the Academy did two decades ago resulted in a publication, *Blueprint for Bibliography,* that was included in a compilation of classics in information science of the last 150 years. As practitioners, our *Environmental Periodicals Bibliography* is, to the best of our knowledge, the most cost-effective search tool built upon human and computer interaction. It offers high information content and can be searched both in print and on-line.

On the former college campus where the Academy is located there have been created and published more different kinds of information services in print and electronic form than have originated from any other place in the world. ABC-Clio Information Services, located there, has been the womb from which the Academy's knowledge of bibliography and information dissemination have sprung. The Information Institute can and does tap the expertise of seventy persons at ABC-Clio whose educational backgrounds include Ph.D.s, J.D.s, and degrees in library and information science, and in business, and whose experience spans all levels in business and academia. Their insights form a part of the work and aspirations of the International Academy's Information Institute.

The mission of the Information Institute is subsumed under the topic "Transition to the Information Society: Challenges, Opportunities and Policies." Of the three program areas identified—education, research and dissemination, and transition policies of the private and public sector—we have focused most heavily on the first. We are now nationally recognized as a change agent in education for the Information Age.

We seek answers to questions that are of serious concern to many who try to lead us toward the Information Age. Our initial educational efforts are directed to providing answers to the following two questions:

> First, where and how will the broad-gauged information professional of the future be educated?
>
> Second, where will today's decision-makers, the principals in our various enterprises, gain the expertise they need to deal with rapid technological changes and their impact on people, an impact that becomes more critical with the rapidity of change that characterizes the Information Age?

The first question relates principally to new programs in higher education, the second to a wide array of purpose-built and tailor-made continuing education and staff development programs.

Today, if an enterprise[1] seeks to employ a lawyer, an accountant, or an engineer, it is clear at which professional school such trained individuals may be found. Similarly, a data processing person, a librarian, or a MBA graduate can easily be identified with specific educational programs. If, however, leaders in the enterprise have come to recognize that all information functions should be guided by a new kind of professional, one whose integrated education includes:

1. information science,
2. computer science and data processing,
3. communications and telecommunications,
4. management of information systems,
5. records management, and
6. systems and management studies,

then they cannot find a graduate or professional school whose graduates have experienced systematic educational exposure to these converging subjects.

Rapid convergence of technology and practice in the real world of enterprise has not yet led to a corresponding convergence in either academic or in-house education. The Information Institute's educational rationale is based on the proposition that persons are needed with a breadth of knowledge in the six subjects listed above. An appropriate integrated educational program does not exist today, not because it is not needed, but because the several graduate programs that do exist teach only a part of the essential curriculum. These programs still respond to educational perceptions of past decades rather than to current or future needs.

Anyone who has had an insight into enterprises can tell you horror stories of waste and confusion, about "information pathology," situations arising from lack of breadth or inadequate skills, or decisions made with yesterday's inadequate knowledge tools. We hope we can explore at this conference the potential contribution of a new integrated program for information science or "information resource management," designed to cure the information pathology from which today's enterprises suffer. The problem is not how to create such a program, because it exists in embryonic form or in parts, but how to accelerate the change processes in existing educational enterprises. Educational institutions may wish to examine models that they can consider for adoption. My own perception of the situation suggests that a new integrated master's program is needed in information science or information resource management. In our effort to call attention to needed breadth we certainly do not wish to neglect the depth required for a full curriculum. If a new M.A. program evolves, its curriculum should be reviewed in the context of the continuum that may include both undergraduate programs in "information literacy" and appropriate Ph.D. programs.

Deep concerns about relevant educational philosophies and the nature of future curricula are reflected in a substantial amount of work now being done on individual campuses and in professional associations. In my particular knowledge universe I can think of the work done in library associations and, more extensively, in ASIA (The American Society for Information Science) and ALISE (The Association for Library and Information Science Educators) whose President, Jane Robbins-Carter, is with us at this conference.

To the best of my knowledge only two enterprises outside the educational establishment are involved in addressing the information pathology of which I speak: IBM, currently with a $25 million commitment, and the Information Institute of the International Academy. Although considerably less than $25 million, our commitment is nonetheless wholehearted. The office of the IBM Director of University Relations is currently engaged in an initiative to which leaders of enterprises can look with appreciation. IBM has made an offer to graduate schools of business and management intended to lead to the selection, in April 1985, of up to twelve such schools, each to receive two million dollars (of which one million dollars is in IBM hardware), plus an unspecified additional amount of software. We await with great interest the proposed plans of these schools. In particular, will programs emerge with sufficient breadth—that is, with what we call integrated education, including all educational streams necessary for a well educated information professional?

Meanwhile, the Information Institute will proceed with its initiative, which commenced at its May 1982 Conference on Education for Information Management (held jointly with the Association for Library and Information Science Educators and chaird by Dean Michael K. Buckland). We have continued with other co-sponsored conferences and activities. The Emporia Conference is the fifth such activity in the last two-and-a-half years. Dr. Philip N. James, the newly appointed Director of the Information Institute and Vice-President of the International Academy, who is present at this conference, will continue to give these program endeavors of the Information Institute priority consideration. I anticipate that with insights we have gained, we shall be seeing an acceleration of our involvement in integrated educational programs for information professionals. This conference will, we hope, make significant strides in that direction.

On the second educational question that the Information Institute is addressing, as to where today's decision-makers will gather the Information

Age expertise they need, I see an array of diagnostic, consulting, continuing education, and staff development and training programs evolving in which the Information Institute might serve as the hub of a substantial network of concerned and expert participants and institutions.

New perceptions of an integrated information function in enterprises call for rigorous analyses of the effectiveness of present processes, needs assessments, and other diagnostic processes. It is clear from our conversations with heads of enterprises that they recognize a need—indeed, often suffer from a malaise on problems of adapting to the Information Age. It must be noted that the enterprises whose principals do not feel such a need may be the real candidates for diagnostic aids: those in greatest need of help!

As part of our diagnostic process, for example, we anticipate looking at each enterprise very much as if it were a physiological system. We will apply the insights of James Grier Miller, developed in his magisterial work, *Living Systems.* Dr. Miller, who is associated with the Information Institute and who is regretfully absent from this conference because of an illness, has shown us useful analogies between an organism and an enterprise. Examining the neurological functions of an enterprise, its information flows and disruptions both within the enterprise and from outside sources, can produce useful insights. Our examination may turn up, for example, inadequacies in tapping external information from the knowledge environment. Fenwicke W. Holmes, the President of the Academy (who is also at this conference), has addressed this problem in his avant-garde thinking, reflected in his recent speeches and in a conferences sponsored by the Information Institute and the Santa Barbara Chamber of Commerce in May 1984.

The organizers of the present conference have succeeded in bringing together different streams of education and practice. The Information Age needs the educational resources all of you represent, for you each teach valuable course content that is needed by the enterprise of the future. But the graduate schools need to go through a faster metamorphosis, to minimize the present waste and confusion in enterprises.

The Information Institute of the International Academy plans to continue to stimulate the current processes of change and reappraisal, helping to direct education in various streams toward a new integrated information science or over-arching information resource management field. We shall continue to serve as a change agent, and now look to preparing educational models for the future. We also plan to be more actively involved in clarifying the roles that broadly educated information professionals can play and in defining the skills they need. Opportunities for growth are available to those of you who can develop a truly integrated program. The Information Institute has developed a multi-disciplinary expertise in its now substantial professional and business network, and will continue to serve in relating the different streams of education and practice to each other. The huge challenges of the information age provide all of us with extraordinary opportunities to be of service to our society.

NOTES

1. I gratefully acknowledge that the cue for the use of the word "enterprise" in this context comes from a paper by Marilyn M. Parker (IBM Corporation, Los Angeles Scientific Center, 11501 Wilshire Blvd., Los Angeles, CA 90025), "Information Management for Enterprises. A View of the Future," March 1984. The word "enterprise" is used here as a generic term, broader than "organization," or "business," or "institution," including "government" and "academic institutions" as well.

The dictionary (Merriam-Webster) defines "enterprise" as:

1. A project or an undertaking that is difficult, complicated, or risky, or
2. (a) A business organization, or (b) a systematic, purposeful activity.

PART I

FOUNDATIONS AND CONCEPTS

Roger C. Greer

A Model for the Discipline of
Information Science

THE PROBLEM

Bell,[1] Naisbitt,[2] Toffler[3] and others writing about the post-industrial Information Age have stressed the significance of information as the dominant social commodity in this period of human history. Occupations associated with the acquisition, storage, retrieval and dissemination of information are assigned social responsibilities unimagined in pre-1956 society. Although we are more than a score of years into the information age, the information professions remain in an uncertain, uncoordinated and unplanned state of development. Without an overall conceptual framework, specific information related activities cannot be generally defined in relation to societal processes of information transfer. Perspectives of much of the information community remain focused inward toward a "... rationalization of each immediate technical process..." reinforcing Pierce Butler's[4] 1933 lament. Meanwhile, the compelling need for consensus on allocations of public resources, a broad research agenda, responsive programs of education and activities appropriate for each information profession is compounded daily by the unprecedented rate of societal change. This paper proposes a conceptual framework for the information professions, a research agenda and implications for the education of information professionals.

PURPOSE

The purpose of this paper is: (1) to identify a common core of functions, roles, objectives and activities of all the information professions; (2) to propose a research agenda of sufficient breadth to yield a practical, coherent theory base for all the information professions; (3) to define the activities associated with this research and theory development as "information science"; and finally, (4) to suggest implications for the education of information professionals.

DEFINITIONS

In order to communicate the level of conceptualization intended in this paper, some operational definitions of commonplace terms are necessary:

Knowledge is an awareness of reality contained within an intellect. According to Boulding[5] ". . . knowledge is what somebody or something knows, and that without a knower, knowledge is an absurdity."

Information is recorded knowledge, i.e. knowledge external to an intellect. Information may be reconverted to knowledge when reassimilated by an intellect.

Data are unprocessed symbols. Data are the raw materials of knowledge. When processed by an intellect and recorded, data become information. Machine processing of data is controlled by the intellectual content of the software.

Communication consists of a sender, message, medium and receiver.

Information transfer is that part of the communication process wherein the message is recorded and received by one or more individuals.

Information profession is an occupation whose basic commodity is information, and whose purpose is that enhancement of the information transfer process among specific clients through the design and management of databases and information organizations.

Information science is the academic discipline from which the information professions derive their theoretical base. Mason and Swanson[6] assert that, "The principal objective of science is to explain, account for, or predict empirical phenomena by means of laws and theories." The responsibility for predicting or accounting for empirical phenomena by means of laws and theories is appropriate to the discipline from which the information professions derive theory.

THE PROBLEM AMPLIFIED

At the present Stage of the Information Age there appears to be a continuous stream of conferences organized to serve the interests of specific groups of information workers. These groups may be sub-groups of conventional library science, e.g. The Public Library Association of the American Library Association, or new groups whose organizational genetics are derived from and molded by new developments of information technology, e.g. On-Line Searchers and Data Processors. There are also explosive developments among groups that may have existed under many different labels but are emerging as significant new information professions, such as Informationa Managers, Records Managers, Information Resource Managers, Managers of Information Systems, Managers of Decision Support Systems, Archivists. A significant and logical consequence of the current stage of self-awareness of many of these emerging information professions is the need to assemble to discuss common problems, e.g. optimal techniques, procedures, organizational status and training.

The impetus for organizational genesis is frequently provoked by this need for recipe level solutions to practical problems.[7] The assumptions motivating conference planning activities spring from a belief that one's peers possess and will share this knowledge. Conferences provide the structure wherein speakers are rewarded through recognition of their leadership by peers and working colleagues. While this level of interaction is reasonable and even necessary to the development of a particular information field, it also contributes to a cycle of shop-level discussions, conferences and publications. Research efforts and subsequent reports are often oriented to operations issues to accommodate the needs and interests of practitioners. In this cycle, the quest for a generalizable body of theory is neither provoked nor pursued.

If theoretical solutions are sought from fields outside a group's area of interest, attention is focused upward to the lore and literature of parent fields of origin or location, e.g. business, public administration, engineering, or education. In general, it is reasonable to suggest that no significant body of research on issues confronting information professionals has developed within these parent fields. More often than not, because these information groups are recent creations of the information age, their existence as a professional group is neither acknowledged nor wholly accepted by the broad fields from which they evolved.

Simultaneously, separate information groups appear to ignore each other except to emphasize their differences. Acknowledgement of the possibility that other information workers may be members of the same species and possible possessors of useful knowledge, or are at least seeking answers to similar problems, is uncommon. The consequence of this occupational parochialism is a commitment of enormous redundant energy to the narrowest aspects of information work. From the narrow perspectives of specific types of information systems operating in specific environments, the possibility of the emergence of a broad theory based research agenda is remote. The absence of this unifying research and theory base contributes to the uncertainties of direction and general fragmentation of educational and training programs for the information professions.

The ubiquitous pressure of change is a fundamental characteristic of the Information Age. The growing number of information workers and increasing significance of their function in society compels articulation of the scope of this area of human endeavor. To do this, it is necessary to develop a systematic program of research and education common to all components of the field. This can be achieved by drawing all information professions together within a framework consisting of an academic discipline representing the core of theory common to all. From this core, each professional field of activity may devise appropriate application. In this way, the information professions would relate to the discipline of information science as social work relates to psychology, law and public administration relate to political science, business to economics and medicine to biology.

CHARACTERISTICS COMMON TO
ALL INFORMATION PROFESSIONS

A beginning for this articulation of information work must start with an analysis of the functions, objectives, activities and techniques of all information groups. An examination of the work of these groups suggests a core of four characteristics common to all. Broadly stated, these four categories are:

1. Responsibility for the design and management of an information system encompassing a database;
2. Responsibility for the design and management of an organization consisting of staff, equipment, space and financial resources to provide the interface between the information system and the potential user;
3. Responsibility for accomodating the information needs and behavioral characteristics of a specific client population;
4. Responsibility for the commodity "information" and the objective of enhancing the processes of information transfer.

ACADEMIC DESIGNATIONS FOR
THE FOUR CHARACTERISTICS

Before attempting a detailed description of some of the obvious components of these four fields, it is useful to assign labels consistent with the academic perspective. Since each field falls within the scope of activities and interests of a larger framework of disciplines and professions, terms drawn from this academic base and combined with the modifier *information* contribute to a recognition of conceptual roots and linkages with other segments of academia.

Database design and management requires the appropriate application of technology to the acquisition, storage, retrieval and dissemination of information. An appropriate designation for this activity is INFORMATION ENGINEERING. The *American Heritage Dictionary* defines *engineering* as "the application of scientific principles to practical ends as the design, construction, and operation of efficient and economical structures, equipment, and systems." The current use of the term *information science* for this area of information work is unfortunate for two reasons: (1) First, it restricts the scope of the science of information to a narrow aspect of information work associated with the storage and retrieval of information and the automation of aspects of library work. Computer scientists (or more appropriately computer engineers) restrict the scope of information sciences even further to the design of equipment and related software. Neither of these narrow attributions of the label suggests the inclusion of human or social behavior except in a peripheral way such as man-machine interface studies. (2) Secondly, by defining the term *information science* narrowly and relating it to a specific aspect of professional work, the information professions are denied the use of this term to identify the discipline supporting all. This leaves only the weaker and less descriptive label *information studies* to identify the core information discipline. From a practical point of view, the amorphous *information studies* places the discipline within the family of *studies* such as American Studies, Asian Studies, Women's Studies, etc., rather than among the bedrock disciplines such as Sociology, Economics, Political Science, etc. The consequence is an unnecessary hurdle for this new discipline to win a seat at the academic table.

Management and management science is an area common to all professions and enterprises requiring an organization of staff, space, equipment and operating funds to accomplish a specific purpose in society. Each field must draw upon theories, techniques and practices of management and modify them to fit its purposes. For example, business enterprises must make modifications in the theories to fit the objectives of producing products and profits; similarly, public administration must fit these theories to its objectives of service; likewise, educators must orient these theories to objectives associated with the processes of teaching and learning.

In the same way, the information professions must draw upon management theories and modify them to accomplish the objective of enhancing information transfer. INFORMATION ORGANIZATION MANAGEMENT is the field responsible for managing resources to create data bases and deliver information services to a client population.

The study of human behavior associated with the activities of acquiring, processing, storing and utilizing information must draw heavily upon the behavioral sciences and may properly be labeled INFORMATION PSYCHOLOGY. In addition, this field must address the human impact of various information formats and characteristics of information systems and information technologies. Thus, while drawing upon existing research in other fields, information psychology must develop a new theory relating human behavior to information transfer.

The study of the role of information in society and the systems, processes and pattersn of information transfer must draw its perspectives from the discipline of sociology. This field, which may be labeled the SOCIOLOGY OF INFORMATION must address issues associated with the creation of knowledge and the various social systems involved in its dissemination and utilization.

Although each field is distinctive enough to be considered separately, it is also evident that their interrelationships are profound. No single field can be adequately understood without consideration of the impact of the others. In other words, the objectives of enhancing information transfer held by the information engineer and information organization manager influence and are influenced by the sociology of information and information psychology. In combination, these four fields encompass the aspects of information transfer (or inhibited) by a mediating information system. It is suggested that the label for the discipline encompassing these four fields should be INFORMATION SCIENCE.

A HIERARCHY OF CONCEPTUALIZATION

The four fields represent a hierarchy of conceptualization. The sociology of information takes the broadest perspective of the role of information and the processes of information transfer in society. Information psychology narrows its perspectives to human behavior associated with information transfer. Information organization management restricts its scope to organizational design and management of information systems. The narrowest or most specific perspective is taken by the field of information engineering because of its responsibility for database design and management. This conceptual hierarchy is reflected in Figure 1.

Figure 1

A conceptual hierarchy of the four fields of information science

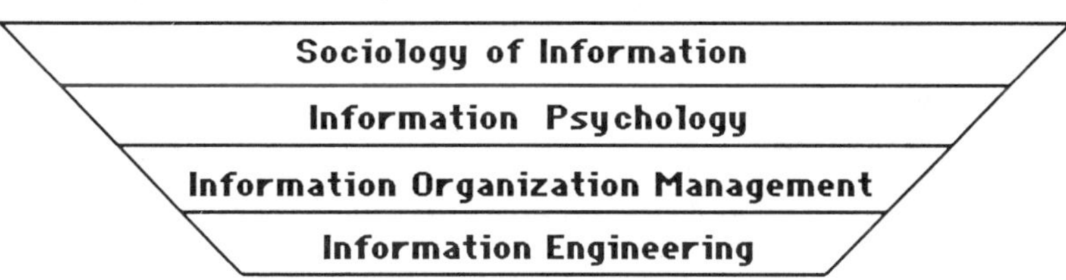

While the scope of these separate fields narrows from societal to database issues, they remain integrated and interdependent. The activities of each of the information professions from librarian to information

manager to archivist are further restricted in scope by environments, formats, objectives, etc. However, each information profession must derive its rationale for specific functions from the four fields defined above.

A PROPOSED RESEARCH MODEL

Each field contains a series of interrelated steps or processes associated with its role in information transfer. These processes are influenced by external factors of environments, such as language, and values, and legislative policy. A research agenda oriented to the study of these influences and the circumstances of predictability could yield a body of generalizable theory relevant to all information professions. Therefore, an examination of the dynamics of each field can be undertaken by an analysis of: (1) the *processes* associated with each of the four fields; (2) *the environmental and policy context* which influences and is influenced by each field; and (3) the existing *theory and research methodologies* for studying the relationships between and among the processes and the environmental and policy variables. Figure 2 is a representation of these three components of the research model. This representation is presented in detail for each field in Appendix 1.

Figure 2

A research model for information science

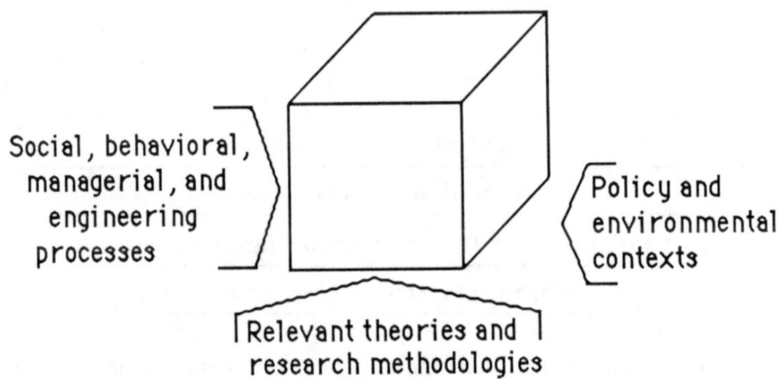

The model employs a three-dimensional cube to indicate dynamic interaction. While the cube is useful in displaying interaction it also implies sharp delineations and straight lines which is not wholly accurate.

THE SCOPE OF THE FOUR FIELDS
OF INFORMATION SCIENCE

A preliminary analysis of the four fields yields an initial list of distinct processes for each field. The policy and environmental context remains for each field while relevant theories and research methodologies vary with the focus of a field. The following is a detailed description of these components for each of the four fields.

INFORMATION ENGINEERING

Design and Management Processes

Specific processes identified as essential to the design and management of databases are:

1. Needs assessment—the analysis of the information needs and behaviors of the client population being served by the database;
2. System design—planning and designing the architecture of a database oriented to the needs and behaviors of the client population;
3. Identification of relevant data/information for potential inclusion in the database;
4. Data evaluation and selection—analysis of quality and relevance of specific data/information for inclusion in the database;
5. Data/information acquisition—the process of acquiring materials from a vendor or publisher or inputting data to a computer;
6. Organization of data/information for storage—cataloging/programming;
7. Retrieval of data/information;
8. Repackaging or reorganizing data/information;
9. Dissemination or delivery of information to clients;
10. Discarding/withdrawing of data/information from the database.

Policy and Environmental Context

The engineering processes associated with the design and management of a database are influences by a variety of variables external to the organization. These variables are categorized here as environmental and social context. The specific variables identified within this category remain constant for all four fields, i.e. the level of conceptualization and the terms used for this category are intended to convey a societal perspective. The level of conceptualization may be narrowed to reflect the immediate context of each field of activity. However, this approach would seem most useful to an applied research effort. A societal perspective for all four fields is essential for a general theory based on research agenda. The initial list of variables which appear to have obvious influences on the processes and are themselves influenced by the processes of the four fields must include the following:

1. Culture—language, philosophical and moral values, educational system, concept of time, etc.;
2. Physical geography—aspects such as climate and topographical characteristics;
3. Political structure of society—the system for governance and underlying values regarding the role of government in a dynamic society;
4. Legislation and regulations issued by legislative and regulatory agencies of government;
5. The economic system under which the culture functions;
6. Technology—the level of sophistication in terms of computer and telecommunication technology;
7. Information policy—copyright laws, policies regarding secrecy, censorship, privacy, the public's right to know and government responsibility to inform.

It must be emphasized that the application of the processes and the influence of the policy and environmental variables would vary from culture to culture or country to country. Consequently, theory must be limited by its cultural context unless multi-cultural research is undertaken.

The Relevant Theory Base and Research Methodologies

A research program for this field should begin by drawing upon the existing theory and research methodologies developed in other academic disciplines and research fields. A systematic analysis of research in these fields could provide a tentative theory base from which a research agenda could develop. The research methodologies employed by these fields may be utilized until appropriate modifications or new techniques are developed. The relationship between the processes and the policy and environmental variables must be understood for the development of a general theory of value to all information professions. Current theory and research methodologies developed by other fields must be examined for relevance and utilization. An initial list of these disciplines and fields should include the other three fields of information science because of their interdependent relationships discussed earlier. Other disciplines to consider in an initial list are suggested below.

1. Sociology of information;
2. Information psychology;
3. Information organization management;
4. Operations research;
5. Networking theory;
6. Communication theory;
7. Information processing theory, including artificial intelligence;
8. Classification theory.

INFORMATION ORGANIZATION MANAGEMENT

Management Processes

The processes associated with the management of an information organization are collapsed into eight broad categories:

1. Define the mission of the organization;
2. Assess the information needs of clients;
3. Define objectives for the organization;
4. Develop policies, strategies and procedures;

5.   Implementation of plans;
6.   Operation and supervision of the organization;
7.   Feedback and evaluation;
8.   Modification.

Policy and Environmental Context

The processes associated with the management of an information organization, as with the processes of informatjon engineering, are influenced by, and in turn, influence the variables identified as constants of the policy and environmental context. (See Appendix 1, Figure 4, for a representation of these variables.)

Relevant Theory Base and Research Methodologies

A research agenda for this field must incorporate the theories and research methodologies developed in other management oriented endeavors. In addition, the theory generated by the other fields of information science are essential to an examination of this field. Listed below are some of the fields to be included in this category:

1.   Information engineering;
2.   Information psychology;
3.   Sociology of information;
4.   Organization theory;
5.   Systems theory;
6.   Change theory;
7.   Sociology of the professions.

It should be noted that professional practice of the information professions is associated with the processes of information organization management and information engineering. Research programs in these fields would necessarily have a direct relevance to practice, reflecting Barnard's dictum that the best theory is the most practical.[8] The influences of data bases and information organization on how individuals, groups and society in general access, process, utilize and transfer information must be accounted for in a theory of information science. Pierce

Butler argued for this objective over 50 years ago when he observed that "Any understanding of society must include an understanding of this social element and all of its functions in communal life."[9]

INFORMATION PSYCHOLOGY

Information professionals operate information systems in order to enhance the information transfer processes of a specific client population. This goal requires (1) a knowledge of existing theory regarding human behavior associated with information, (2) an assessment of the needs and behavioral characteristics of the specific population being served. Information psychology is the field of information science concerned with the development of this theory. In other words, information psychology must serve the information professions as educational psychology serves the field of education. The scope of a research agenda for this field may be suggested by a series of questions about behaviors.

Behavioral Processes

1. How does a person decide that there is need for information? What are the conditions or motives that provoke this awareness?
2. What processes are involved in decisions to satisfy or ignore the need?
3. What are the strategies employed in searching for information and how does this differ among individuals?
4. What are the variations in behaviors associated with the search for information? How does the configuration of the information system used affect these behaviors?
5. What methods and criteria are employed in evaluating the relevance of information acquired?
6. What are the behaviors associated with the processes of assimilating information? How does format and system design affect this aspect of behavior?
7. What cognitive styles are employed in information processing?
8. How do individuals organize, store and retrieve information from memory?

9.   What are the varieties of forms and pattersn of information
     utilization?

Although considerable research has been done on many of the questions posed above, little systematic effort has been made to pull this
research together for information professionals.

Policy and Environmental Contexts

The impact of policy and environment on behavior associated with
the questions identified above appears to be profound. How behavior
is modified by these variables singly and in combination is of fundamental significance to an information professional designing services
for a client group. (See Appendix 1, Figure 5, for a representation of
this relationship.)

Relevant Theory Base and Research Methodologies

Appropriate academic and research fields from which to draw relevant
theory and appropriate research methodologies must include the following:

1.   Information engineering;
2.   Information organization management;
3.   Sociology of information;
4.   Social psychology;
5.   Behavioral psychology—personality theory, perception theory,
     motivation theory, attitude theory, cognitive science, theories
     of intelligence, role theory;
6.   Psycho-linguistics;
7.   Physiology;
8.   Religion;
9.   Educational psychology.

SOCIOLOGY OF INFORMATION

The final and broadest field of concern to the information professional
relates to the role of information and the processes of information transfer

in the development and dynamics of a society. The scope of this field includes the processes of information creation through the phases of dissemination, diffusion and use. The perspective remains societal throughout. The social processes identified within this field are reflected in the following questions:

Social Processes

1. What are the patterns of knowledge creation?
2. What are the systems for recording knowledge?
3. What are the mechanisms for the mass production of information?
4. What varieties of systems are employed in the dissemination of information?
5. What systems for bibliographic control of the records are being produced in society?
6. What is the paradigmatic structure for the organization of information by subject fields?
7. What are the patterns of diffusion of knowledge?
8. How is information used in society?
9. What systems exist for the preservation of information?

Policy and Environmental Context

Each of the societal information processes must be examined to determine the who, what, where, why and how they have been influenced by the policy and environmental context in which they occur. Once again, the contextual variables are represented in Appendix 1, Figure 6.

Relevant Theory Base and Research Methodologies

Considerable study and current interest in the issues associated with the sociology of information is manifesting itself in the social sciences, from sociology to economics. Some of the fields appropriate to the study of the sociology of information are:

1. Information engineering;
2. Information organization management;

3.   Information psychology;
4.   Economics;
5.   Intellectual history;
6.   Political theory;
7.   Cultural anthropology;
8.   Sociology—sociology of knowledge, symbolic interactionism;
9.   Cybernetics;
10. Bibliometrics;
11. Socio-linquisitics.

Other fields such as the religion and social psychology are relevant to both information psychology and sociology of information but are listed only in one place. The inclusion of information psychology, information organization management and information engineering in this list as with others is intended to bring the application of these fields with overlapping perspectives.

CONCLUSION AND IMPLICATIONS
FOR EDUCATION

Since Flexner's famous 1910 study[10] on professional medical education for the Carnegie Foundation it has been axiomatic that theory is the backbone of any program of professional education. It is also commonly understood that professional work is the application of theory in the service of society. It follows that any program of instruction for information professionals must draw heavily upon the general theory of information sicence and consider its application to various contexts of professional work. Instruction in technique and procedure is not appropriate for formal degree programs because of two inherent properties, non-generalizability and temporality. Therefore, instruction in techniques and procedures is appropriate to in-service training and programs of continuing education.

The objective of this paper is to demonstrate that there is a common theoretical core for all information professions. In fact, it may be stated that unless an information based activity possesses the four components discussed earlier, it is not an information profession. Currently a core of theory exists in fragments scattered throughout academia. An analysis by means of a conceptual framework suggested in this paper will yield a synthesis of existing knowledge, and a plan for development can evolve. Meanwhile, the basis for a coherent program of education for information professionals in the information age exists and the substance can be structured for specific degree programs.

At present there are separate degree programs at the bachelor, master and doctoral levels in library science. In addition, there are emerging degree programs, certificate programs and collections of courses in information management, information science, records management, archive management, data processing and information systems management. These instructional packages often are grafted on other degree programs in business, computer science, public administration, communication and education. The common element in all these activities is the preoccupation with the applications of computer technologies to the processes of storing and retrieving information. Unfortunately, this common element also limits the scope of many emerging programs.

Since these instructional efforts are responses to a marketplace demand for "trained" information workers, the emphasis tends toward operational subjects and systems concepts. A consequence of this present state of development is that the general state of the educational component of the information professions is a mirror image of the organization and conference planning efforts discussed earlier. It is unlikely that the present piecemeal development of education activities scattered throughout academia will evolve in broad theory based on curricula providing support and unity essential for the development of all the information professions.

Although the primary focus of this paper has been toward the development of a research agenda, the flip side of this agenda must be a rational educational structure. The four fields representing the scope of information science embody the theory base for the information professions. As information sciences is an academic discipline, it is possible to project a sequence of degree programs based on the four fields and originating within the social sciences. These programs should include the bachelor, master and doctor of philosophy sequence similar to other academic fields. Each of these degrees would approach the four fields from a different perspective. The bachelor's level would strive for breadth through topics associated with the policy and environmental context. The master's degree would approach each field from the perspective of the processes while building on undergraduate studies. The doctor of philosophy must approach each field from the perspective of the theory base and research methodologies while building upon the bachelor's and master's curricula.

By drawing on a common theoretical core in the four areas, parallel terminal professional degree programs at the master and doctoral levels can be developed for practitioners. The bachelor in information science would be generic to all fields. Separate professional master's degree programs in library science, information management and management information systems could share a common core and build toward specificity in the application of theory in each of their environments. Doctoral level programs could serve the need for advanced education for upper level practitioners.

Currently, academic administrators show little interest in drawing together the energy, talent and activities of information-oriented faculty in a new concentration to achieve an organizationally viable critical mass. Nevertheless, this concentration would appear to be essential to the necessary development of theory and its applications in the linkage of academic and professional education. Such an integration of all components of information based on activity would soon achieve public recognition of its significance and create its own momentum toward developing the field. If we fail to case our net widely and commonly draw it in, society will move inexorably toward Daniel Bell's predictions of an information rich and information poor dichtomy in the world.

Figure 3

TOPOLOGY OF THE FIELD OF INFORMATION ENGINEERING

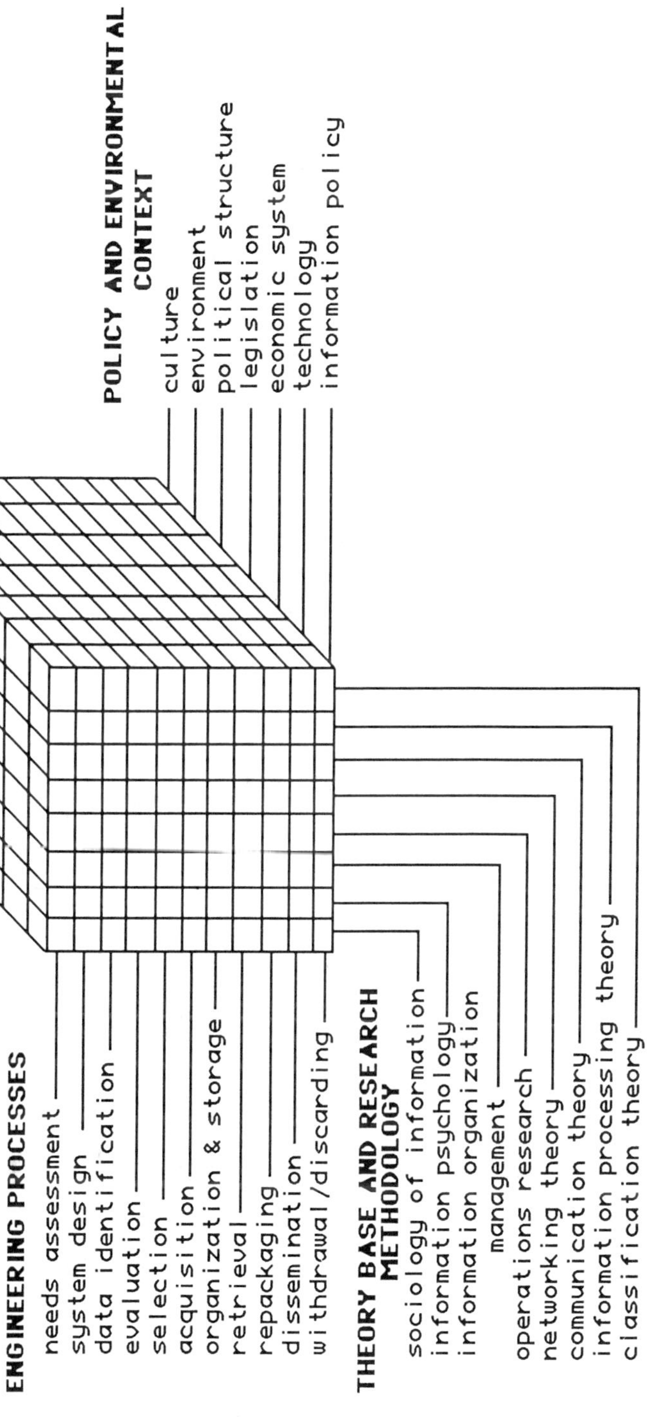

POLICY AND ENVIRONMENTAL CONTEXT

culture
environment
political structure
legislation
economic system
technology
information policy

ENGINEERING PROCESSES

needs assessment
system design
data identification
evaluation
selection
acquisition
organization & storage
retrieval
repackaging
dissemination
withdrawal/discarding

THEORY BASE AND RESEARCH METHODOLOGY

sociology of information
information psychology
information organization
management
operations research
networking theory
communication theory
information processing theory
classification theory

Figure 4

TOPOLOGY OF THE FIELD OF INFORMATION ORGANIZATION MANAGEMENT

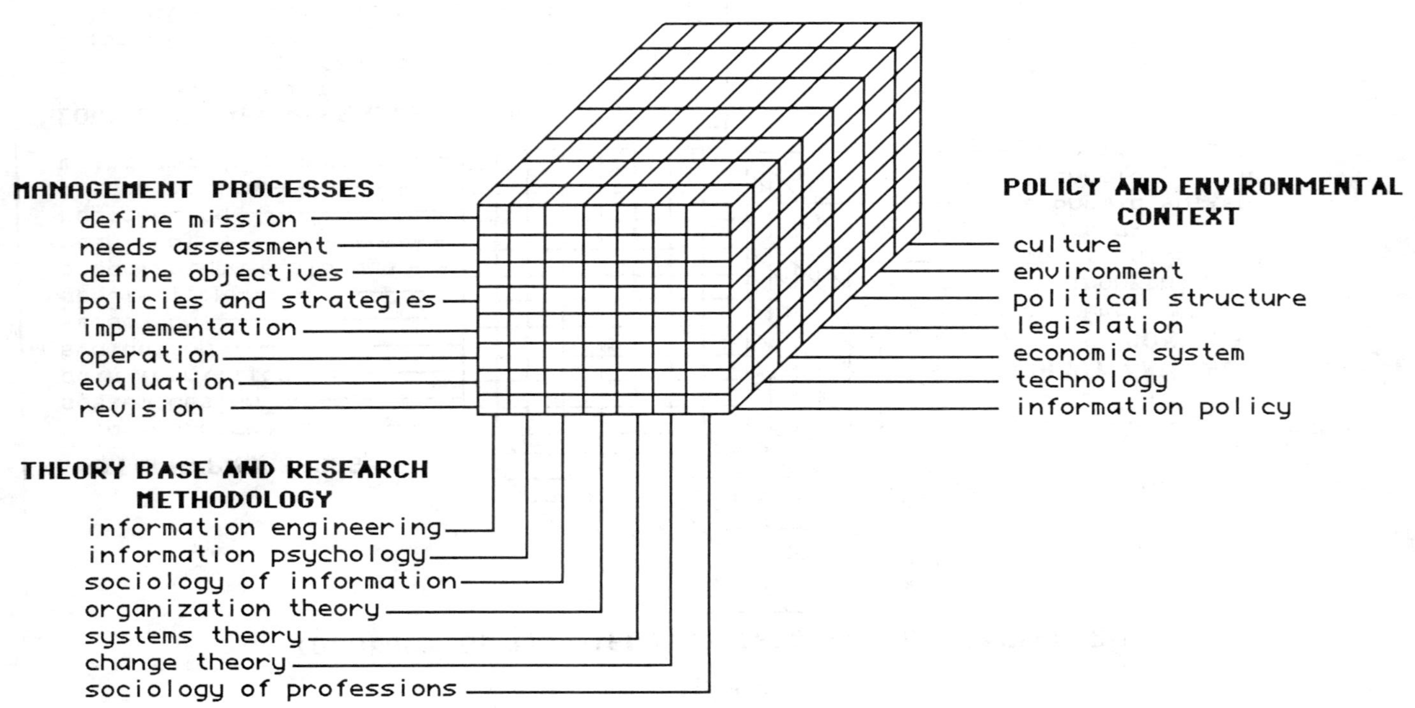

Figure 5

TOPOLOGY OF THE FIELD OF INFORMATION PSYCHOLOGY

BEHAVIORAL PROCESSES
awareness of need
action decision
strategies for search
behaviors in search
evaluation
assimilation
processing styles
memory
utilization

THEORY BASE AND RESEARCH METHODOLOGY
information engineering
information organization
management
sociology of information
behavioral psychology
psycho-linguistics
physiology
religion
educational psychology
social psychology

POLICY AND ENVIRONMENTAL CONTEXT
culture
environment
political structure
legislation
economic system
technology
information policy

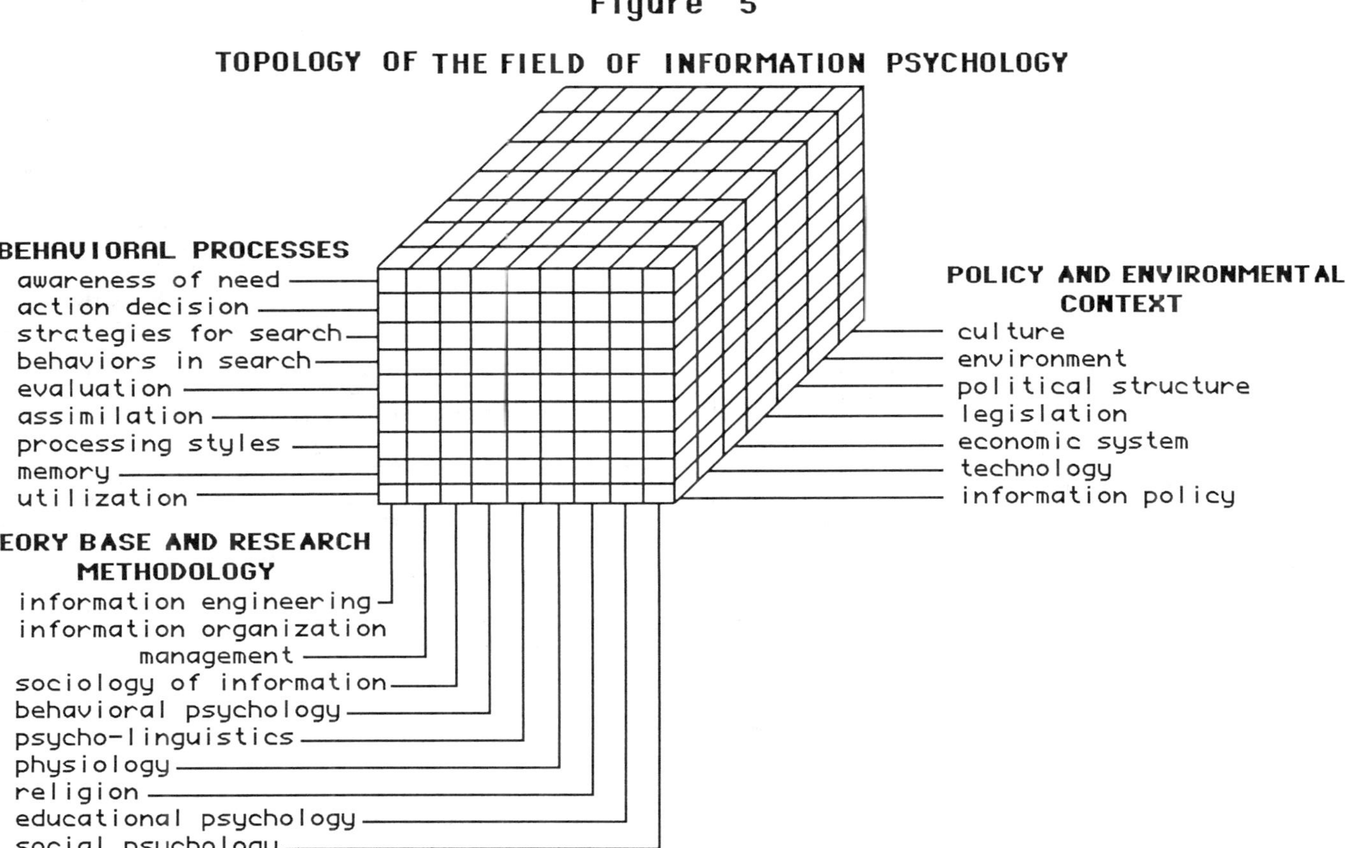

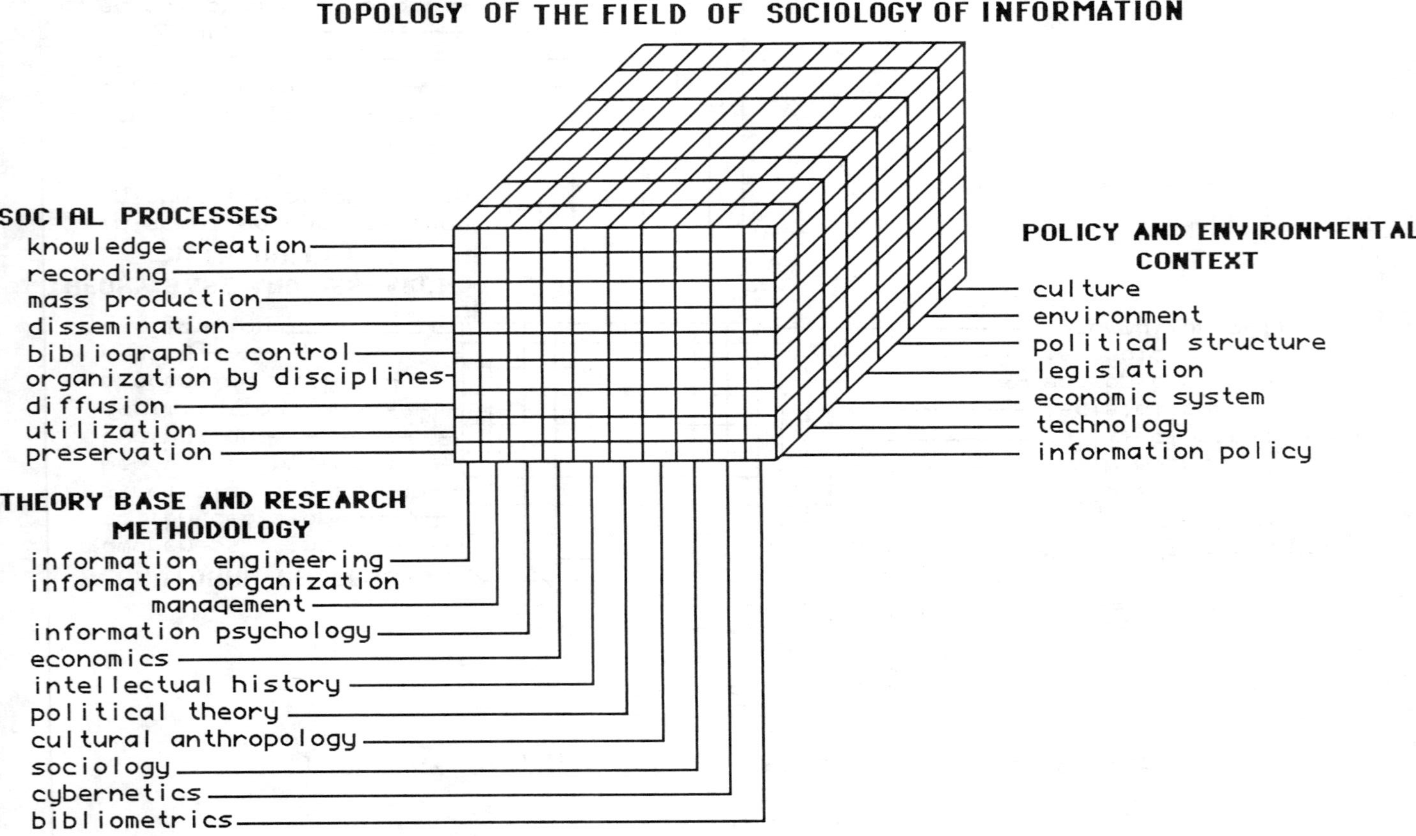

Figure 6
TOPOLOGY OF THE FIELD OF SOCIOLOGY OF INFORMATION
SOCIAL PROCESSES
knowledge creation
recording
mass production
dissemination
bibliographic control
organization by disciplines
diffusion
utilization
preservation
THEORY BASE AND RESEARCH METHODOLOGY
information engineering
information organization
management
information psychology
economics
intellectual history
political theory
cultural anthropology
sociology
cybernetics
bibliometrics
POLICY AND ENVIRONMENTAL CONTEXT
culture
environment
political structure
legislation
economic system
technology
information policy

NOTES

1.   Daniel Bell, *The Coming of the Post-Industrial Society: A Venture in Social Forecasting,* New York, Basic Books, 1973.

2.   John Naisbitt, *Megatrends: Ten New Directions Transforming Our Lives,* New York, Warner Books, 1982, 11-38.

3.   Alvin Toffler, *The Third Wave,* New York, Wm. Morrow, 1980.

4.   Pierce Butler, *An Introduction to Library Science,* Chicago, University of Chicago Press, 1933, xii.

5.   Kenneth Boulding, *The Image: Knowledge in Life and Society,* Ann Arbor, University of Michigan Press, 1956, 16.

6.   Richard O. Mason and E. B. Swanson, *Measurement for Management Decisions,* Reading, Mass., Addison-Wesley, 1981, 12.

7.   Michael Huberman, Recipes for Busy Kitchens: A Situational Analysis of Routine Knowledge use in Schools, *Knowledge: Creation Diffusion, Utilization* (June 1983), Vol. 4: 478-510.

8.   Chester Barnard, *Organization and Management,* Cambridge, Harvard University Press, 3.

9.   Pierce Butler, *op. cit.,* xi.

10.   Abraham Flexner, *Medical Eduction in the United States and Canada: A Report to the Carnegie Foundation for the Advancement of Teaching,* New York, Carnegie Foundation for the Advancement of Teaching, Bulletin No. 4, 1910.

E. Burton Swanson

INFORMATION SYSTEMS: NECESSARY FOUNDATIONS

INTRODUCTION

Information systems is a young field of study, and a general consensus as to its appropriate foundations has yet to emerge with clarity. However, from the research of the past decade or so, it is possible to draw some conclusions about the consensus which should eventually be reached. In the present paper, I venture a few such conclusions.

Three fields of study—computer science, management science, and organization science—are proposed as necessary foundations. Each of these fields focuses upon certain foundational elements held to be themselves necessary for the study of information systems. The identification of these elements, and the rationale for their necessity as foundations, constitutes the principal body of this paper.

The three fields proposed as necessary foundations correspond closely to those from which MIS research has to date been drawn in an ad hoc manner. (Hamilton and Ives, 1982, and Culnan, 1984.) All three are candidates as "reference disciplines." (Keen, 1980.)

I should emphasize, however, that the view to be expressed is my own, and no doubt reflects the usual biases (which I hope will be transparent to the reader).

In the discussion which follows, I will generally equate the term "information system" with "management information system" ("MIS"), and accept the definition of an MIS as "a computer-based organizational information system which provides information support for management activities and functions." (Ives, et al., 1980.)

NECESSARY FOUNDATIONS

The recent emergence of the information systems field has been most obviously associated with the growth of computing in organizations. Indeed, a preoccupation with computers is typical among information system professionals. For many, therefore, information systems is essentially a form of applied computer science.

Computer science obviously provides the technological basis for the study of information systems. Insofar as one accepts (as I do) that information systems incorporate computing and communications artifacts as necessary components, one must admit that the foundations for the design of these components originate fundamentally in computer science.

Three subjects of computer science—data, software, and hardware—are of particular interest to information systems, and will be discussed in turn. Each is an important foundational element, it is argued. (It is recognized that the distinctions between the three elements are not sharply drawn, but it is hoped that this does not detract for present purposes.)

The study of *data*—their logical structure and organization, and their physical storage and retrieval—is currently at the core of computer science work. (See, e.g. Codd, 1982.) This was not always the case, however. Data were originally neglected by computer scientists in favor of computational procedures, and have come to currency only with the rise of large scale data bases integrated from individual data files common to business data processing.

As a foundational element in the information systems, data thus have a substantial history, viewed in terms of the evolution of business data processing technology.

Data, and data bases, are necessary as an information systems foundational element for one overriding reason, viz. that it is by means of data that the basic facts of any organization are established and employed.

Recorded data are not theoretically understood to presuppose some data model, which provides the semantic architecture required for interpretation and hence, manipulation. (Fry and Sibley, 1976.) Because such semantics necessarily confront issues of usability, i.e., adequate representation from the user's view, data models are of interest beyond the relatively narrow confines of computer science. However, as formal structures, they are housed principally in this field.

Reflecting the importance of data and data bases as foundational elements, approaches to information systems development have been increasingly centered in these terms in recent years. (See, e.g., Chen, 1976 and Zachman, 1982.)

The study of *software* is necessary for the field of information systems for several reasons, two of which are emphasized here. Perhaps the most important reason is that application software incorporates the formal information processing procedures of the organization. Specifically, application software specifies *a priori,* the manner in which certain data of the organization are to be interpreted and acted upon. This specification is embodied by the conditional choice structure of the software, as represented for example, by a program designed to classify a set of transaction data presented to it, and intitate another, new set of transactions accordingly.

Thus, software incorporates important decisions made by the organization with respect to its data. These decisions are, in effect, made in advance of the data to be presented, and thus absorb the uncertainty associated with their processing.

Secondly, as a reason for its foundational importance, software is necessarily constructed (and often used) by means of an information processing language. "Higher order" languages are those tailored to classes of information processing problems of the organization. A choice among languages thus presents a practical, yet subtle problem to the organization, individually and collectively.

For this reason, the study of information processing languages is fundamental to the study of information systems. And, the individual acquisition of a language skill adds fundamentally to the repertoire of technique which may be applied to the information processing problems of the organization. (Condescending attitudes toward those who read and write in such languages are not only unwarranted, but are genuinely dysfunctional with respect to the communication processes necessary to support organizational information processing.)

Finally, it should be noted that software development and maintenance is now a major organizational enterprise, with substantial resource implications. (Boehm, 1981, and Lientz and Swanson, 1980.) For this reason too, it is a significant foundational element.

Hardware, as a foundational element, today plays a less conspicuous role in the study of information systems that in earlier years. Its importance, relative to software, has receded to the point where many now consider it to be "merely packaging."

It would be a mistake to underestimate hardware, however. First and most important, users of information systems interact with data and software *only* by means of hardware. (Even the printed report employs "hard copy.") In a sense, then, the packaging is not removable, and the medium strongly shapes the message.

For this reason, hardware will always be of importance to information systems. (There is, for example, substantial current interest in human factors engineering in the interaction between the computer and its user, as represented by a recent international conference on the subject, the first of its kind. See Interact '84.)

The advent of personal computing provides a particularly illuminating example of the enduring importance of hardware as an information system foundation. In earlier times, users were insulated from classical parameters of computing technology, such as memory size, disk capacity, number of storage drives, and printer speed. Now, however, with the distribution of full sytem computing to the individual office, users have begun to speak in the familiar vocabulary of the manager of data processing. (One may reasonably feel reassured, as well as discomforted, by this development.)

We turn next to a consideration of the foundational elements to be found in the field of management science.

Management science as a field of study provides important normative foundations for information systems. Its principal concerns (from this author's perspective) are with problems, models, and solvers. Problems are understood to range from unstructured to structured, and to involve processes of intelligence, design, and choice. (Simon, 1960.) Models are the product of the design process, and provide closure with respect to problem contexts. Solvers provide means of choice examination and resolution for classes of models. (The distinction between models and solvers is adapted from Geoffrion, 1984.)

The study of *problems* is fundamental to information systems, in that information is classically understood to be of relevance only in a problem context. (The study of information economics, as developed by Marschak, 1968, and others is the exact embodiment of this presupposition.)

Of particular currency is the subfield of decision support systems (DSS), which is in fact defined in terms of the type of problem resolution supported (semistructured to unstructured, according to author. (See, e.g., Keen and Scott Morton, 1978.)

Also of interest is the management support system (MSS) concept advanced by Geoffrion (1982), which is defined in terms of the support of structured problem resolution, in contrast to DSS.

The notion of the level of problem addressed, e.g. strategic, management control, or operational, as distinguished by Anthony (1965), has also been fundamental to information systems theory, in terms of frameworks proposed, e.g., by Gorry and Scott Morton (1971), and provides further evidence of the importance of the problem construct, as an information systems foundation.

Models are also of fundamental significance as a foundational element. This significance stems from their formal role in problem representation, which allows their incorporation into software and data, discussed above.

Models express the relationships which are asserted to hold (or be held) among the data of the organization. (For example, that the level of a production output is constrained according to the machine capacity allocated to it.) Models, like data, thus provide important semantics for the information systems in which they are employed.

Of particular current interest in the field of information systems is the establishment of a modeling framework which provides for management science models, an architecture equivalent to that provided by data models for data bases, as discussed above. The "structured modeling" approach recently proposed by Geoffrion (1984) is particularly promising in this regard.

Solvers provide the computational technology by means of which models are addressed and explored. They include two familiar types: algorithms and heuristics. The former have long been a major subject of methodological research in management science. The latter are becoming of increasing importance, however, especially with the development of expert systems which incorporate the "rules of thumb" common to the "knowledge base" of the sophisticated decision maker.

Solvers, like the models to which they are applied, are therefore important elements of information systems designed to support organizational decision making, and are likely to be of increasing significance with the advances in artificial intelligence expected over the years to come.

We consider next the field of organization science and its foundational elements.

Organization science, more generally referred to as organization theory, provides important descriptive and explanatory foundations for the field of information systems (in contrast to the normative foundations provided by management science, as characterized above.)

Three organizational entities are viewed here as important both to organization science, and to information systems: individuals, organizations, and institutions. The necessity of each as a foundational element is argued next.

The study of *individuals,* specifically their behaviors and attitudes as organizational participants, is a principal endeavor of organization science, and a central concern of many information systems researchers.

Perhaps the most important class of individual studied, in an information systems context, is the system user. "Implementation research," in particular, has sought to explain individual user behavior in terms of a number of "success factors." (For a useful review, see Lucas, 1981.)

Designers of information systems have also been a subject of study, especially as contrasted with users in terms of individual characteristics such as psychological type. (Mason and Mitroff, 1973, and Gingras and McLean, 1982.)

The study of cooperative units of individuals, i.e. *organizations,* is seen as necessary for the field of information systems for two distinct, but complementary reasons. First, information systems are ostensibly designed to serve organizational purposes. Put otherwise, information systems are typically to provide organizational functionally first of all. (Indeed, when implemented, they are ultimately functionally absorbed into the organization's fabric, in a process of mutual adaptation.)

Thus, an information system is from one point of view an organizational component, with no identity independent of this context. Perceived in this way, an information system may not be studied except by means of organization theory. (The author is sympathetic to this particular view. The reader will note that the rationale presented in support of *all* the foundational elements discussed in this paper is essentially an organizational rationale.)

Secondly, information systems are themselves the products of organized endeavors. The organization responsible for this endeavor, which consists of the design, development, implementation and maintenance of the information systems portfolio of the host organization, is the information systems organization.

As information systems portfolios have in recent years accumulated, there has also been a concomitant development of the information systems organizations as a major functional unit in the host organization served. This rise to prominence has generated much interest in the study of information systems organizations, as important organizations in their own right.

Organizational science further concerns itself with the study of *institutions,* social patterns of interpretation and behavior reflecting the stable, cultural norms prevailing within a particular organization, or across organizations. (The term "culture," currently in high fashion in organization theory, may be substituted for present purposes, if desired. For a useful review of the culture concept, see Smircich, 1983.)

Institutions give shape to formal organizations, and are in turn shaped by them. (No organization can be divorced from its culture, nor can cultural development be halted. By the same token, cultural content is malleable, with diffusion from within and without. As described by Zucker (1984), this may be a useful perspective from which to view the introduction of microcomputing in organizations.)

The necessity of the institutionalist perspective in information systems is argued effectively by Kling (1980), who contrasts it with various forms of "systems rationalism" (with traditional emphases on goals and tasks, formal organization structure, participant needs and rewards). An example of the application of this perspective is the notion of the "web model of computing" described by Kling and Scacchi (1982), where the formal organizational system is generally eschewed by the analyst, who focuses first of all on the straightfoward empirical question, "What kinds of things do people do here?"

In summary, organizational science focuses upon three entities—individuals, organizations, and institutions—all of which may be seen to play crucial foundational roles in understanding information systems.

CONCLUSION

The discussion of the necessary foundations for the study of information systems is summarized briefly in Table 1. Three related fields of study —computer science, management science, and organization science—are identified, together with three foundational elements in each case, for a total of nine elements overall. It has been argued that each of the nine elements is necessary in establishing the foundations for a theory of information systems.

TABLE 1

Necessary Foundations of Information Systems
Summary

Foundational Field	*Foundational Element*
Computer Science	Data
	Software
	Hardware
Management Science	Problems
	Models
	Solvers
Organizational Science	Individuals
	Organizations
	Institutions

The acceptance of the necessity of three kinds of study—organizational science, management science, and computer science—as foundations for the study of information systems, has clear implications for educational programs in the I.S. field, in particular.

The three supporting fields may be likened to the support system of a simple, three-legged stool. Each leg is required to support the weight to be imposed upon the stool. Significantly, two legs (management science and organizational science) are most often positioned within a management (or business) school (typically spanning more than one department). The other (computer science) is placed elsewhere, typically in a letters-and-science or engineering school.

The overall implication is that, however an information systems program is formally organized within a university, it should establish strong intellectual associations with the three foundational fields described above. Failure to do so invites fundamental weakness.

Are the three fields sufficient as foundations for the development of the information systems field? Here there may be substantial debate. My own view is: in the short run, yes. In the long run, no.

In the short run, there is much to be exploited by building on the three necessary foundations discussed here. The information systems field is very young, and little weight has been imposed as yet upon the three-legged stool. New programs of study in information systems, in particular, can be usefully "bootstrapped" from one or more of the three foundational fields.

In the long run, however, it will probably be necessary to draw more diectly from other underlying foundations. The three immediate foundations rest themselves upon more basic foundations in the social sciences, mathematics, and engineering. Numerous opportunities exist to build directly from research in these areas.

Foundations in philosophy and the systems sciences are also of substantial long run importance. Concerns with regard to the former have been expressed in a recent colloquium. (See "Information Systems Research: A Doubtful Science?") For a basic treatise on systems science and its philosophical foundations, an especially helpful work is Churchman (1971).

Lastly, steps toward the integration of the information sciences may also be critical. Currently, for example, the information systems field is little concerned with documents (as opposed to data). However, document processing will play an increasingly significant role in organizations in the coming years, as word processors evolve into support systems of much greater sophistication. The document, historically the subject of study of the library and information sciences, may thus become a necessary foundational element for information systems as well.

In conclusion, drawing more directly from the more basic foundations, and striving toward the integration of the information sciences, in addition, should deepen the intellectual content of the information systems field, in the long run. It may also be necessary to establish information systems as a mature area, one which contributes to its immediate foundations, in return, in addition to drawing from them. Many of us who have been involved with information systems research over recent years look forward to this day, in particular.

REFERENCES

Anthony, R. N., Planning and Control Systems: A Framework for Analysis. Boston: Harvard University, 1965.

Boehm, B. W., Software Engineering Economics. Englewood Cliffs, N.J.: Prentice-Hall, 1981.

Chen, P. P., "The Entity-Relationship Model: Toward a Unified View of Data," ACM Transactions on Database Systems, Vol. 1, No. 1 (March 1976), pp. 9-37.

Churchman, C. W., The Design of Inquiring Systems: Basic Concepts of Systems and Organizations. New York: Basic Books, 1971.

Codd, E. R., "Relational Database: A Practical Foundation for Productivity," Communications of the ACM, Vol. 25, No. 2 (February 1982), pp. 109-117.

Culnan, M. J., "The Intellectual Structure of Management Information Systems, 1972-1982: A Co-citation Analysis," unpublished working paper, revised August 10, 1984.

Fry, J. P. and Sibley, E. H., "Evolution of Data-Base Management Systems," Computing Surveys, Vol. 8, No. 1 (March 1976), pp. 7-42.

Geoffrion, A. M. "A Management Support System for Distribution Planning," INFOR, Vol. 20, No. 4 (November 1982), pp. 287-314.

Geoffrion, A. M. Structured Modeling and Aggregation, University of California, Los Angeles, unpublished manuscript, 1984.

Gingras, L. and McLean, E. R., "Designers and Users of Information Systems: A Study in Differing Profiles," Proceedings of the Third International Conference on Information Systems," Ann Arbor, 1982, pp. 169-181.

Gorry, G. A. and Scott Morton, M. S., "A Framework for Management Information Systems," Sloan Management Review, Vol. 13, No. 1 (Fall 1971), pp. 55-70.

Hamilton, S., and Ives, B., "Knowledge Utilization Among MIS Researchers," MIS Quarterly, Vol. 6, No. 4 (1982), pp. 61-77.

"Information Systems Research: A Doubtful Science?," IFIP W. G 8.2

Colloquium, 1-3 September 1984, Manchester Business School, Manchester, England, Proceedings to be published by North-Holland Publishing, Amsterdam.

Interact '84, 1st IFIP Conference on Human-Computer Interaction, 4-7 September 1984, Imperial College, London, England, Proceedings to be published by North-Holland Publishing, Amsterdam.

Ives, B., Hamilton, S., and Davis, G. B., "A Framework for Research in Computer-Based Management Information Systems," Management Science, Vol. 26, No. 9 (1980), pp. 910-934.

Keen, P. G. W., "MIS Research: Reference Disciplines and a Cumulative Tradition," Proceedings of the First International Conference on Information Systems, Philadelphia, 1980, pp. 9-18.

Keen, P. G. W. and Scott Morton, M. S., Decision Support Systems: An Organizational Perspective. Reading, MA: Addison-Wesley, 1978.

Kling, R., "Social Analyses of Computing: Theoretical Perspectives in Recent Empirical Research," Computing Surveys, Vol. 12, No. 1 (March 1980), pp. 61-110.

Kling, R. and Scacchi, W., "The Web of Computing: Computer-Technology as Social Organization," Advances in Computers, Vol. 21 (1982), pp. 1-90.

Lientz, B., P., and Swanson, E. B., Software Maintenance Management. Reading, MA: Addison-Wesley, 1980.

Lucas, H. C., Jr., Implementation: The Key to Successful Information Systems." New York: Columbia University Press, 1981.

Marschak, J., "Economics of Inquiring, Communicating, Deciding," American Economic Review, Vol. LVIII, No. 2 (May 1968), pp. 1-18.

Mason, R. O. and Mitroff, I. I., "A Program for Research on Management Information Systems," Management Science, Vol. 19, No. 5 (January 1973), pp. 475-487.

Simon, H. A., The New Science of Management Decision. New York: Harper & Row, 1960.

Smircich, L. "Concepts of Culture and Organizational Analysis," Administrative Science Quarterly, Vol. 28, No. 3 (September 1983), pp. 339-358.

Zachman, J. A. Business Systems Planning and Business Information Control Study: A Comparison," IBM Systems Journal, Vol. 21, No. 1 (1982), pp. 31-53.

Zucker, L. G., "Microcomputing as Institution Building," Computers and Information Systems Colloquium, University of California, Los Angeles, 31 May 1984.

Richard O. Mason

THE VALUE OF INFORMATION

TOWARD A MODEL OF VALUES AND COSTS

In the later years of his life, Jacob Marschak worked in the field of information economics (1968). Much of his work is mathematical and precise and is primarily applicable to technical designs. His overall framework, however, is quite broad and reveals the basic relationships that a designer must take into account in deciding on information and its delivery. A modified version of Marschak's model is summarized in Figure 1.

This model reflects two of the economic considerations in the design of an information system. At the outset, data requirements are identified and the form, amount, precision, and other attributes of the data are specified. Then the data is collected. This involves physical and mental processes which extract sensations from the outside world and form them into data. This task is performed by a Collection Function. Resources are consumed whenever data is collected and, thus, a Collection Cost Function is required to estimate Data Collection Costs.

The resulting data is then transmitted to one or more processing points where it is analyzed, calculated, compared, formatted, and converted into information. If appropriate, the information is stored in the system's memory for subsequent retrieval. When information is required, either on a demand pull basis or system triggered push basis, it is transmitted to one or more users or decision makers. This is accomplished by a Transmission and Processing Function which also requires a Transmission and Processing Cost Function.

The recipient now takes in this information and interprets it. The information is either ignored or used. Frequently the information simply entertains or educates the recipient and, thereby, changes his psychic state. Sometimes, however, the information produces a change in the recipient's behavior and causes him to choose from among alternative courses of action. This converting of information into new cognitive states or into action is accomplished by a Decision and Use Function. The associated Decision and Use Cost Function also yields a Decision and Use Cost. Parenthetically, it should be noted that many designers overlook these decision and use costs in their analysis. From a social point of view, however, these costs may constitute a major part of the total costs. For example, user-friendly systems minimize decision and use costs by properly relating the information and its means of access to the recipient's preferred patterns of use.

Information use next generates real world actions which, in turn, impinge on actual states and events. This engagement of action with reality produces a Resultant Outcome. A Value Function or a Utility Function associates the Resultant Outcome with the Total Costs required to produce it. The result is the Total Value as determined from the point-of-view of the individual(s), organizations, or social unit involved. The primary task of the information systems designer is to maximize the Total Value of the information system.

In order to evaluate alternative information systems architectures, the designer must be able to *measure* its activities. In particular outputs, inputs and productivity should be assessed (See Mason 1978, Mason and Swanson 1981). But we must also go beyond these activity measures to measure the value of the overall information event as well. That is, it is *not* enough to know that a report on student enrollment, for example, were delivered to the Vice President of Student Affairs at a cost of $75 including one person hour of direct labor, 10 minutes of computer-printer hook-up time, and an accrued charged for data base and computer processing. In addition we want to know whether the provision of this information had any bearing what-so-ever on the V.P. Could he use it? Now? Later? Was he able to make better decisions? Did it improve his understanding of the student enrollment issues he faced? Did he enjoy reviewing it? These questions take us beyond considering information as an object—that is, something tangible or intangible that can be known or perceived by the mind—to considering the *relationships* between the object and the individual or societies who are effected by it. This is the problem of valuation and, as we will see, there are many different ways in which we may conceive of the value of information. The information systems, designer, de facto, bears the responsibility for initiating the process of valuation.

The object to be valued is the information itself plus a concoction of people, procedures and machines which manipulate it. Out of a morass of possibilities available to them, designers must find a way to provide primarily that information which is important to their client and to shunt that which is not. For this the guiding concept is purpose. In what ways does the information system serve the purposes of the broader social system in which it is embedded? One of the best ways to answer this question is to examine the uses to which the information is put.

On Use

Use is that mysterious process by which something is put to a given purpose as a means to accomplish an end. Values flow as a result of accomplishment. But, information, like energy, has both a kinetic and a potential state. That is, it can be in motion and actively stimulating users or it can be at rest, yet still coiled, like a spring, and waiting to be released. When information is in use its impact is direct and usually observable although the chain of events it initiates may take long periods of time to play themselves out fully. When it is at rest its impact can only be inferred from its position and condition. Yet information potential may have enormous value to users because it enhances their capability to accomplish their ends.

Thus, the use value of information has two components:

1. *Actual use*

2. *Potential use*

The value of information is actual when the information is used directly in making a decision or arriving at a judgment. For many systems, however, this is a small portion of the value. A library or a large database, for example, may contain many items that are rarely, if ever, accessed. So, how can they be of value?

Information is valuable in a potential sense if it builds the users' capability to respond effectively to situations which are likely to arise in their environment. An executive who is negotiating a deal with another company, for example, is better prepared if she has cost figures and "what if" analysis on possible options. When the other company makes an offer she can assess immediately what its impact will be on the firm. The night before the negotiation there are hundreds of counter offers the other company might make. If she has information about each and has an idea about its relative attractiveness to her firm, she is prepared. During the course of the next day's negotiation meeting, however, only a very few options will be actively considered. Does this mean that the effect undertaken to collect and analyze information about the hundreds of other options was wasted? The answer, of course, is usually "no."

If there is a reasonable likelihood that the information might have been used effectively then it has potential value although it doesn't have actual value. Moreover, if the failure to provide the information would have caused a loss or an embarrassment for the negotiator—a condition referred to as "regret" by Leonard "Jimmie" Savage (1972)—it also has potential use value. So, in effect, both those items of information that were actually used and those that had a potential of being used possessed value.

A similar circumstance occurs in libraries. Book usage often follows Pareto's law, about 20% of the books in the collection account for about 80% of those checked out and used. Some books are never checked out. The question arises, "Should these unused books be discarded or sold?" The answer is, "It depends on the policy, strategy, and purpose of the library." If the library is a public library and the book is an older novel it is likely it should be purged. It is not providing a service to the public as evidenced by its lack of use. The space, time, and other resources used to retain the book on the shelves could likely be used more effectively elsewhere. That is, if we assume that the novel is not scarce (that is, it is replaceable) and that the entertainment value lost by failing to provide it to a future borrower is small, the opportunity cost of retaining the idle book is high. Consequently, its potential value to the public and to the library is low.

Let's say, by way of contrast, that the idle book is the only known copy of a research monograph and that the library is a university library. Then the book should probably be retained. Academic libraries generally perform a repository function and safeguard existing knowledge that might prove useful in the production of additional knowledge. Consequently the academic library would be remiss in its duty if it knowingly discarded knowledge that might be of use to future generations of knowledge seekers. So although this dusty old monograph does not have actual use value it may have very high potential use value.

Several points emerge from these illustrations of the woman negotiating for her company and of the library reviewing its collection.

1. The value of the information is intrinsically linked to the policy, strategy, and social purpose of the system possessing it. That is, the information used should serve the goals of the institution.

2. The value of the information lies in the capacity it creates for the system which possess the information to respond effectively—that is, to achieve its goals—at some future date. This future date, as in the case of the library, might be decades or even centuries in the future. This is the fundamental notion underlying the concept of potential use value.

3. Opportunity cost or loss is the appropriate concept for making a valuation as revealed in the following decision analysis.

Common sense tells us that if the value in use and the opportunity loss estimates are high then a relatively low likelihood of information being demanded justifies the decision to retain it. Mathematical analysis supports this view. Specifically, information should be made available whenever Probability (information needed by user) $\dfrac{B + D}{A + B + C + D}$

Where:

+A   = Value in Use
−B   = Opportunity Cost of Resources
−C   = Opportunity Loss
+D   = Value of Reallocation

In the illustration discussed above the negotiator placed a high value on the information that was actually used (i.e. value in use, variable A)

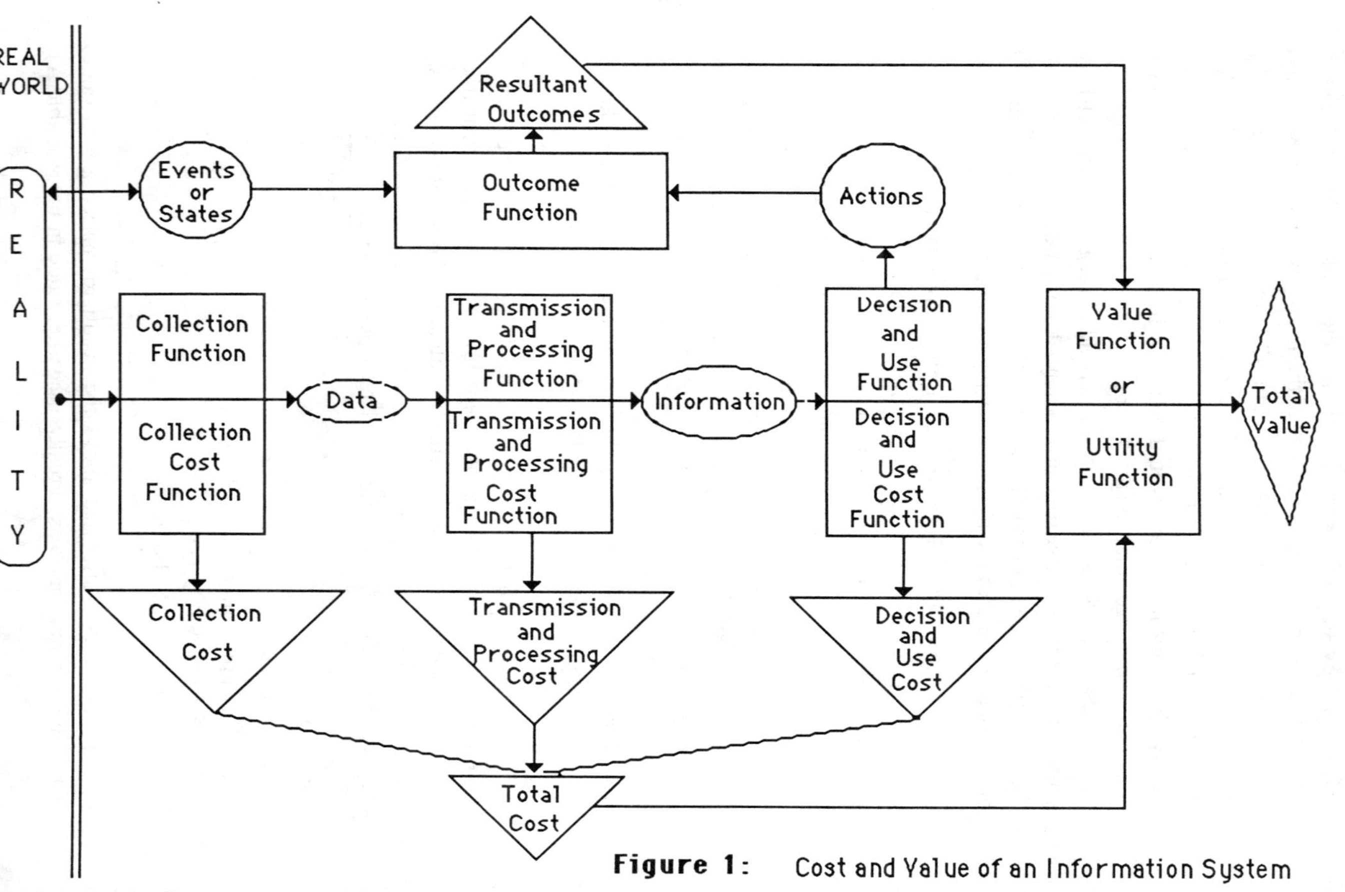

Figure 1: Cost and Value of an Information System

State of Information Use
Information Decision
Information Needed By User
Information NOT Needed by User
Information Made Available
Information NOT Made Available
Value in Use
A
An Information Success
Opportunity Cost of Resources Tied-up
B
An Information Waste
Opportunity Loss is NOT Being Able to Respond
C
An Information Failure
Value of Reallocation of Resources
D
An Information Success

Figure 1A

and was concerned about the opportunity loss she would have experienced had she failed to acquire the information before coming to the bargaining table (i.e. opportunity cost). Accordingly, even a relatively low probability of demand justified making the information available. The same type of justification applies to the academic library although the values are expressed in social terms rather than in financial terms. If the library possess the only surviving copy of the monograph then one might argue that the opportunity loss or the regret involved in failing to preserve it approaches infinity. This derives from a belief that a civilization should retain its knowledge and not destroy it. As a result almost any non-zero probability of demand justifies making the information available. Arguably, such is not the case with the public library and the unused book of replaceable fiction. It's just a little entertainment for someone if read; but, no one is hurt much if it's not available. And yet it is tying up capital and valuable shelf space. Consequently, even a relatively high probability of demand may not justify its retention. This is not to suggest, however, that scientific data is inherently more valuable than fiction. (*Moby Dick* beats most research monographs on almost any scale.) The example was merely chosen to illustrate a point.

To summarize: The task of placing a value on information is to determine both its actual and potential use value. Since information must be collected before it is used, it is potential value that is used in the initial design of information systems.

In general, the potential value of information is determined by the following formula:

Potential Value = Actual Value if used

x

Probability of being used

These ideas can be summarized in the following guideline:

Information should be collected and provided anytime its potential value is greater than its cost of provision

This leads to three essential questions:

A. Value for whom?

B. What theory of value?

C. What are the attributes of information which affect its value?

Let us consider each.

A. *Value for Whom?*

A basic task in the design of an information system is to identify all of the parties who might use the information. These are existing actual and potential users and, of course, must include future generations.

For each potential user the following queries are posed:

1. What questions can be answered or what decisions can be made if the information is provided?

2. How important is it that these questions be answered or decisions made?

3. What social or individual objectives can be met if the information is provided?
   What objectives can *not* be met if the information is not provided?

4. Otherwise, how adversely is the user or the social system affected if the information is *not* provided?

The responses to these questions must somehow be aggregated over *all* potential users. At this point an important choice must be made by the designer. The designer must evaluate the responses either from the standpoint of the individual as an individual pursuing his or her own goals or from the standpoint of the social organization pursuing its collective goals.

Closely allied with the task of identifying the relevant parties is the need to initiate a process by which their individual interests are taken into account. Obviously, the designer can ask the users directly or otherwise allow them to participate in the design process itself. In particular, each potential user can be asked to respond to the four queries posed above. In large organizations and in public information situations it may be too costly to poll each user. Consequently, other tactics must be used. For example, either representatives must be chosen or people must be identified who typify each point of view and subsequently involved in the user requirements setting process.

Once the parties are identified we must turn our attention to the dimensions of value by which we assess their needs.

B. *A Theory of Value*

The Pennsylvania philosopher, E. A. Singer (1979), argued that values do not exist in abstraction but rather are realized through a means-end schema. Churchman (1967, 1979) and Ackoff, (1972) in various writings, have added precision to Singer's insight and summarize it using of four key categories:

1. Economic — The value for possessing adequate means

2. Scientific — The value for possessing knowledge and understanding of relationships between means and ends.

3. Political — The value for dealing with cooperation or conflict among parties who are pursuing different ends within the same environment.

4. Aesthetic — The value for creating new or different ends.

A given item of information may have value in any or all of these categories. They speak to the purposes to which information is put and these values reside in the users and in the user community.

Information has *economic* value when it can be used to improve the material and financial well-being of the user or the using organization. Information used in the marketing, production or finance decisions of a firm, for example, has economic value to that firm. This value is usually measured in terms of a contribution to profit or to cash flow although the governing measure should be contribution to the strategic objectives of the firm. An example may help to clarify the difference.

From its founding, Willard J. Marriott, Sr., stressed the value of customer service at his Marriott Hotels. At the age of 82 he still read every customer complaint card every day. His business philosophy stressed quality in the form of clean facilities and courteous staff. And he used the customer complaint cards to determine how well his hotels were performing. The elder Marriott used the information directly to achieve his quality of service objectives. Only indirectly did it have a bearing on profits or cash flow. But the complaint cards contained information of economic value nevertheless because they aided Marriott in the successful running of his business.

The economic value of information generally takes on one of three attributes:

1. *Efficiency* — this is information that helps the user perform the same tasks better and with fewer resources. Information which helps the user do the same job faster, at less cost or with higher quality, has economic efficiency value. It is information that informs the user how to do the job "right."

2. *Effectiveness* — this is information that helps the user perform a task that he or she was *not* able to perform before. Information, for example, that reveals to a salesman where to find potential clients that he previously didn't know existed has economic effectiveness value. It is information that informs the user how to do the right job.

3. *Responsiveness* — this is information which helps to respond to demand regardless of the efficiency or effectiveness of doing so. The customer complaint cards did this for Mr. Marriott. They had economic responsiveness value because they helped him and his organization to respond to customer's demands for service.

Information has *scientific* or *knowledge* value, generally speaking, when it provides new understanding of its recipients and enhances their capacity to respond effectively to situations in the future. The chief executive officer of a firm, for example, may request reports on details of the business which do not pertain directly to his responsibility. He may subscribe to many different magazines, journals, report services, and newsletters, the majority of which are not directly relevant to the industry in which he is involved. Or, he may even enroll in a course in the classics. This information may not have direct economic value of the firm; but it may serve to give the CEO a depth of understanding about the firm, the world at large, and how they work that improves his ability to make wise decisions in the future.

Some economic scientific information, of course, has immediate economic application. It may be used directly in producing a product or service. Corporate research and development activities are generally undertaken with this purpose in mind.

Most of the information delivered by educational programs must be justified on its scientific and knowledge value. It does not carry with it immediate economic rewards. Rather, educational information is often comprised of facts, theories, concepts, exercises, and experiences which broadens one's understandings of the course subject matter or perhaps of the world in general.

In summary, understanding and information for its own sake may be an appropriate social goal. Information that satisfies this goal takes on scientific or knowledge value.

Information has *political* value when it increases the power of the recipient by helping them bring people together who share a common concern. That is, it aids in forming community or a "polis." The political value of information is that it helps users gain support for achieving their own goals or it helps eliminate barriers or resistance from others.

Information of political value often is used to establish *equity* among stakeholders who are competing in the same environment. Equity information is used to provide equal amounts of access to, or opportunity for, the following: (1) monetary payments, (2) distribution of goods and services, (3) resource allocations, or (4) such other attributes as socio-economic classes served, geographic areas served, price, quality of service reliability.

This means that political information must also deal with the interests, motivations, stakes, and commitments of the parties involved. For this reason it is present in all social systems and is absolutely essential for their leaders. The CEO, for example, must have information about the motivations of the people with whom she or he does business, both inside and outside the firm. Moreover, the CEO should disseminate information and communicate it in a matter which motivates the recipient to take actions which are consistent with the firm's objectives.

Information has *aesthetic* value to the extent that it evokes feelings of beauty or ugliness within the recipient. At a surface level information may entertain in the sense that it captures the user's attention and compels him or her to "attend to it." This minimal aesthetic value is necessary in order for the information to be received at all. Entertainment, of course, may be the only intent for providing some information such as a television show or a price of diversionary fiction. At a deeper level, however, information, in its role as art, can disturb. That is, information can force someone to reconsider their personal goals and objectives. Experiencing some forms of information can call forth something deeper in one's psyche and make one questions who he is and who he has become.

This call for action has important ramifications. Leadership and its underlying moral spirit are often evoked by the aesthetic content of information. The leader sees "what is" and having sensed it is stimulated to develop plans for creating something else. Moral indignation emerges when the recipient see "what is" and feels deeply that "that *ought not* to be so" and then proceeds to do something about it.

Each of these four values may be present in the same item of information even in common situations such as job performance evaluation. Suppose John Smith's performance on his job is reported to his superior by means of an historical chart which compares John's actual performance to the objectives set for him. An illustrative chart is depicted in Figure 2. The chart reveals that after a few periods in which his actual performance surpassed his objective, John's accomplishments have now fallen well below his objectives. It can be interpreted by each of these four value perspectives.

The scientific value of the performance chart lies in what it reveals about the means-end relationship between John and the outputs he is able to generate on his job and what it tells about himself, his ability to perform on the job as defined, and the supportive nature of the work place itself. This chart when related to the superiors' broader knowledge in the field may give the superior a better understanding of the forces at work in the work place and enhance his overall knowledge of the business.

Figure 2

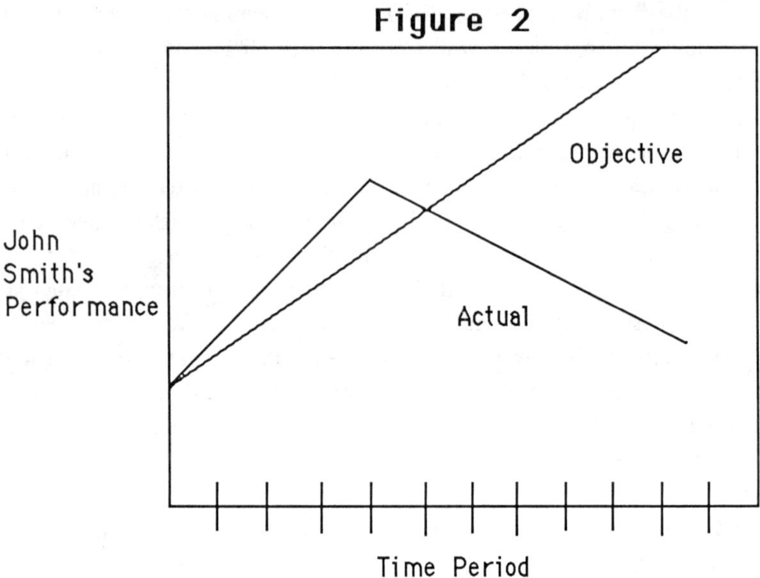

Finally, the chart might inform some very specific economic decisions. John could be fired or he might be sent to a skills training program or new equipment and personnel could be assigned to John to help improve his performance.

As mentioned earlier, the four values just described—economic, scientific, political, and aesthetic—categorize information with respect to the basic purposes of the social systems or of the recipient. Information can also be evaluated in terms of its attributes and role they play in achieving these purposes. For example, we might ask whether John Smith's performance chart is relevant, clear, timely, reliable, valid, or if it has any of a number of other attributes which may effect its usefulness for achieving the recipient's purposes.

C. *Attributes of Information*

Information, like a physical object, is a bundle of attributes. Some of its qualities help recipients achieve their purposes, some may inhibit them. Information which is relevant, for example, but which is also incomprehensible may have little utility although it possesses laudable attributes. Due to this variation in possibilities the task of information systems designer is to insure that the cluster of attributes that characterize the information is appropriate for it's users' purposes. A good place to begin this task is by considering relevancy.

RELEVANCY: THE KEY FACTOR
AFFECTING VALUE AND COST

Relevancy is defined as the closeness of the logical relationship between the information and the use to which it is to be put and is the beginning point for information systems design. Irrelevant information has no value whereas relevant information which relates directly to the solution of the problem at hand has considerable value. It is for this reason that determining relevancy is central to the design of information systems and why establishing it generally requires a joint effort between the users—for whom the information is to be relevant—and the designers. Three interrelated elements are at work here:

1. Information the user *wants.*
2. Information the user *needs.*
3. Information the user is *provided.*

Wants, here, refer to information that is desirable, pleasing or satisfying to users. It may even be entertaining; but, it is not necessarily required by the users to accomplish their job.

Needs, on the other hand, refer to information that has been determined to be essential to the successful execution of the users' jobs. Needs are generally established by means of an explanatory model of the organization's decision and information utilization processes and by means of an analysis of the socio-technical system involved.

The provision of information has two aspects: (1) the information actually provided and (2) the information which it is technologically feasible to provide. The first relates to an evaluation of current systems. The second provides guidance for new designs.

The interrelationship between these three elements and their implications for design can best be understood by examining, in turn, each of eight possible conditions. These logical possibilities have been and are depicted in the Venn diagram in Figure 3.

Figure 3

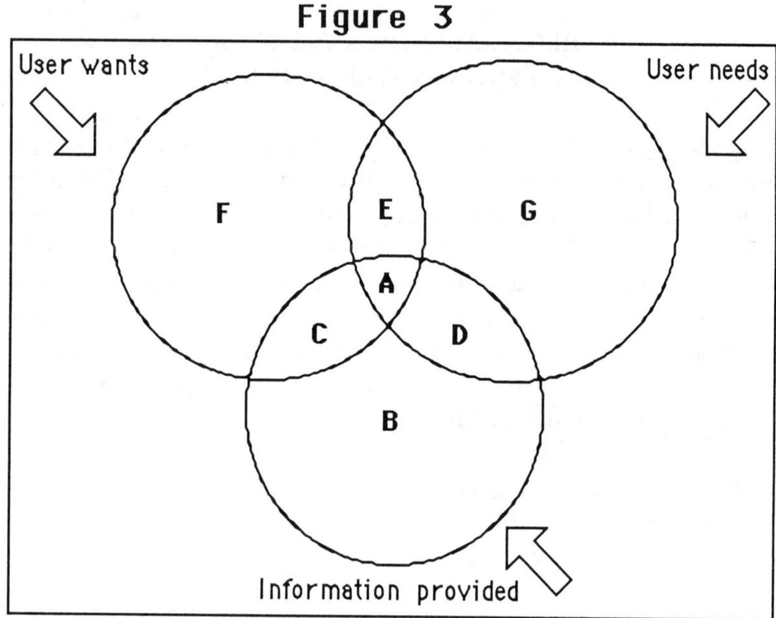

A. *User Wants–User Needs–Information Provided*

Producing this Type A information is the goal toward which all information systems should strive. In this circumstance information is provided which the user wants and therefore will accept and attend to. It is also information which the users need in order to effectively discharge their responsibilities. This is the most relevant information.

B. *User Does Not Want – User Does Not Need – Information Provided*

This is the ultimate of irrelevance and waste. Yet many information systems operate under this condition and information overload results as the recipient becomes mired down with useless information and is distracted and confused. Familiar adages such as "finding a needle in a haystack" and "throwing out the baby with the bath water" apply here because the overloaded user tends to miss, ignore, or throw out Type A information while trying to cope with all of the Type B information. This B condition is so prevalent that it led Russell Ackoff to coin the term "Management Mis-information Systems" to describe it.

Type B is also illustrated by the actions of the president of a large metals manufacturing company. His information systems group had just implemented a budget and control system in which every major sub-unit in the entire world wide organization was established as a cost center. Each of these units had a budget for its various line items of cost. Actual expenditures were then compared with the budget and a variance calculated. Variance over some tolerable limit were highlighted and the responsible parties identified. In total several hundred thousand variances were calculated and reported. The information systems group, full of pride for their accomplishments zestfully prepared a personalized copy of the first report, four inches thick, for the president and presented it to him. To their amazement and utter disappointment, the president took one look at it and threw it into the waste basket. "I never want to see this report again," he said, "It would take me days to read this and I have too many other things to do." He let the group stew for awhile, then he went over to the waste basket, retrieved the document and turned to the group. "You have done a fine job. This information may be useful to many other people in our ogranization. *But this isn't for me!* My needs are simple: Brief readable reports, synopsis data on overall performance and exceptions pin-pointed where there are major trouble areas." What this president wanted in terms of information was buried somewhere *in* the report; but, its relevancy was lost in myriads of irrelevant detail which he did not want and did not need.

C. *User Wants—User Does Not Need—Information Provided*

This Type C condition sometimes arises when users define their own information requirements. It can also result from poor training and a lack of understanding on the part of the user about her job and its demands, or it may result from the failure of the designer to determine requirements properly. There are several important aspects of this condition, however, which bear on the issue of relevance. This condition often arises from conflict or incongruence between the user's goals and those of the organization. Providing some of this Type C information accordingly may appease these users and serve to peak their interests so that they also pay attention to information they need. In extreme cases it may even serve as part of their compensation in the form of a minor fringe benefit. To the extent that Type C information serves to satisfy users and thereby contribute to their overall productivity it assumes relevancy.

D. *User Does Not Want—User Needs—Information Provided*

Under this Type D condition the user is likely to reject or ignore information which is needed to perform the job well. The condition arises from mis-understanding and from the lack of training, especially when a new information systems is installed. In order to avoid this Type D condition many organizations develop education and training programs for the intended users of a new information system.

Types A, B, C, and D refer to successes and failures surrounding information which *is* provided. Types E, F, G, and H, on the other hand, refer to successes and failures created because information was *not* provided.

E. *User Wants—User Needs—Information Not Provided*

This condition reflects a major failure in information provision and should be a prime target for information systems design. Once Type E information is identified then the central design questions become "Is it technologically feasible to provide this information?" (Note that the provision of some wanted and needed information maybe beyond current technological feasibility) and "Is it cost/effective to provide it?"

F. *User Wants–User Does Not Need–Information Not Provided*

This condition may reflect dissatisfied or perhaps even irate users. In some cases their wants may be absurd. The designer can not afford to ignore this condition, however, because the users support for or resistance to the information system often stems from their perception that they are in a Type F information situation.

G. *User Does Not Want–User Needs–Information Not Provided*

This condition has similar implication for design as does condition E. However, it includes an additional design problem, namely to get the users to want the information they need when it is eventually provided.

H. *User Does Not Want–User Does Not Need–Information Not Provided*

An ideal outcome would be to reach the point where only condition A and condition H are obtained. Faced with a situation such as depicted in Figure 3, the designer has served strategies available.

1. Expand the range of wanted and needed information provided until the limit of technological feasibility is met. This requires an increased understanding of the technological options which are available and research and development to produce new options. Figure 4 shows the direction this effort might take.
2. Study user's wants carefully. Then, teach, sell, persuade, bargain or cajole them so that their wants coincide with their needs. One important caveat is in order however: *Users are often the best judge of their needs.* Users usually understand the requirements to succeed in their endeavors better than anyone else, including their

superiors. Well conducted interviews, focus groups, discussions and dialogues frequently serve to eliminate mis-understandings in this area.

3. Analyze and understand users' needs. This is a major undertaking but it is essential. It must begin with an understanding of the total corporate strategy including what business the company is in or is to be in and the kind of company it is or is to be. With a firm grasp of the strategy in mind the designer determines the role played by information services and information technology in it and then maps organizational decision and information utilization processes which links information to strategy. From this analysis a set of rational information needs for each user is determined. In some organizations, needs determined this way are shared with the users in a feedback session in the hopes of creating joint understandings among the parties.

4. Finally, avoid assuming that if users receive the information they want and need, that their decision-making will improve. This procedure assures that relevant information is made available but not that it will be used effectively. "You can lead a horse to water but you can't make him drink."

In this respect Russell Ackoff draws a moral for the designer: "... *it is necessary to determine how well managers can use needed information.* If they cannot use it well, they should be provided either with decision rules or with feedback on their performance so that they can identify and learn from their mistakes." (1967, p. 149)

Having established relevancy the designer may now consider some of the other attributes.

OTHER ATTRIBUTES AFFECTING THE
VALUE AND COST OF INFORMATION

In this book *Organizational Intelligence,* Harold L. Wilensky describes the desirable characteristics of intelligence as follows:

High-quality intelligence designates information that is *clear* because it is understandable to those who must use it; *timely* because it

Figure 4

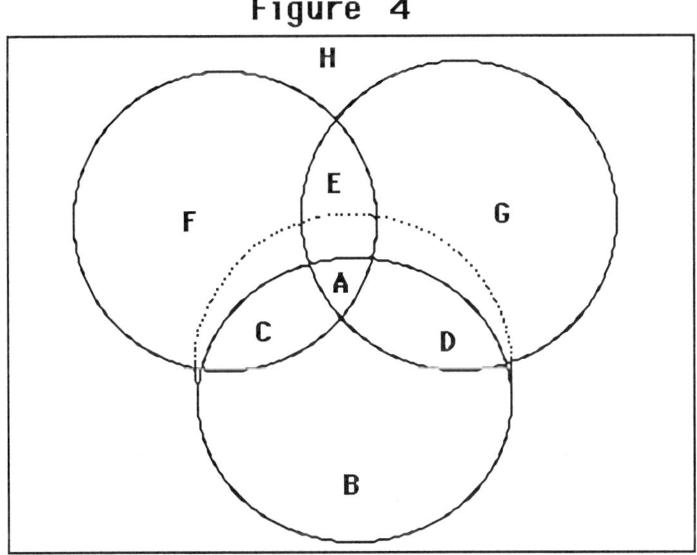

gets to them when they need it; *reliable* because diverse observers using the same procedures see it the same way; *valid* because it is cast in the form of concepts and measures that capture reality (the tests include logical consistency, successful prediction, congruence with established knowledge or independent sources); *adequate* because the account is full (the context of the act, event, or life of the person or group is described); and *wide-ranging* because the major policy alternative promising a high probability of attaining organizational goals are posed and/or new goals suggested. (1967, ppvii-lx)

Each of these attributes—clear, timely, reliable, valid, adequate, and wide-ranging, are generally desirable in information and add value to it. Each, however, has some special aspects to consider.

CLEAR

Clarity is desirable so that the recipient can read the information, understand it and not mis-interpret it. The information should be subject to just the intended interpretation. Consider, for example, the sign which hung at the entrance to a Hong Kong tailor shop: "Customers giving orders will be promptly executed." Does this mean that these Chinese tailors are blood-thirsty merchants or that they are fast and efficient workers?

All information is subject to multiple interpretations. Consequently, the effective designer is one who understands the norms and the point-of-views of intended users and structures the information system accordingly. Sometimes this requires education and joint problem solving. The resulting message is usually simple, uncluttered and to the point. In order to achieve this clarity, a considerable amount of time, effort, and expertise are required. The value of clarity is often underestimated, but, achieving it can also be costly.

TIMELY

Ideally, information appears at the time it is needed or is available shortly before hand. The negotiator described in the illustration above has little value for information she receives after the deal is made. Similarly, a dissappointed borrower has less, if any, value for a book which the library purchases after she has left. Thus, there are critical junctures in decision-making and information use processes at which information has high value. Beyond these points, its value decays, sometimes rapidly. To illustrate in the extreme consider the message. "A missile has been launched which will hit your house at exactly 4:30 p.m. today." Early in the day when there is time for you to hide and to protect yourself, this information has nearly infinite value for you. At 4:30 p.m. its value goes to zero.

Time is always a factor in the value of information but its role is usually not so clear as the preceeding illustration suggests. Some information, like good wine, gets better with age as it assumes new value in the light of history and events. Other information, such as the price of tomatoes today, looses value steadily as time passes, although it may be useful at some later date in a trend or retrospective analysis.

Whatever the time value of information is to the user it generally depends on at least four things.

1. How frequently data is collected.
2. How rapidly it is processed.
3. How quickly the information is available to the user.
4. When, that is what point in time, does the user need the information.

Each of these four conditions have design implications. Continuous and instantaneous sensing of all events means that the data is always available but it also leads to very high costs. Achieving rapid processing and conversion of sensed data into information, however, is generally a technical problem and often may be accomplished by means of telecommunications and computers. Making processed information available to a user is both a technical and an organizational problem and it may require a great deal of effort to achieve.

It is important to realize that speed in one of these steps does not necessarily guarantee speed or timeliness in another. Consider the following sequence:

Event t_1	Event	t_2 Event	t_3 Information	t_4 Information
Occurs $\rightarrow$	Captured $\rightarrow$	Processed $\rightarrow$	Communicated $\rightarrow$	Used

Let us say that the event of interest is the withdrawal of an item from inventory stock. If, as is the case with many inventory systems, a considerable amount of time (t_1) passes before these withdrawal and replenishment events are recorded and made available to the system, then no matter how quickly t_2, t_3, and t_4 are performed, the information is potentially out of date. The result is that it is possible for a user to request the current inventory balance on a video display terminal and receive an almost immediate response on the screen; however, the information it displays will be several minutes, hours, days, or perhaps even months old. As a consequence, the concept of "real time" is only relative to the point at which the information is extracted from in the total chain of production. Real time is not necessarily "real" with respect to current events.

Finally, timeliness is always a function of the needs of the user. Here are two elementary basic design alternatives are available:

1. User *Pull*

    In this design the user's demand governs. The user enters a request into the database or the storage and retrieval system. Design concerns include: how quickly does the system respond with a filled request, (prompt response saves user time and frustration) and how current the information is which is provided.

2. System *Push*

    a. *Periodic*

       This is the design that most accounting and reporting systems employ. Daily, weekly, monthly, quarterly, or annual reports are provided. The concerns are: how often to issue reports (interval) and how long a time period should be covered by the reports (periodicity).

    b. *Triggered*

       This is the design used by exception reporting systems or that results from a "needs to know" analysis. In this design an event such as either running over a cost budget or selling a particular customer a specified product triggers the communication of information. The concerns are: what events should trigger responses and who should know.

RELIABLE

Reliable information is like reliable marksmanship. It is consistent. Whatever biases it incorporates are consistent and therefore may be adjusted for. A scale, for example, may always weigh 5 pounds overweight. If it is consistent (and we know it) then we can subtract five pounds from every weighing to arrive at a correct weight. Reliable informants have the same characteristic. They are people who are neither arbitrary nor capricious. In the same situation they will make the same judgments and report the same information. The costs involved here are the costs of calibration, standardization, and gaining experience with the source.

VALID

Validity is the most difficult attribute to attain and furthermore to know when you have attained it. It requires arriving at the "truth." Ideally, valid information would correspond in all of its important dimensions with reality. Since we can never directly apprehend reality we can only approximate this idea in the limit. Perhaps the most crucial test of the validity of information comes when the information has application and prediction associated with it. If the information "works out," that is, if the application is successful or the prediction is realized, then the information can be considered valid. In the absence of this kind of rigorous pragmatic test information gains validity if (1) independent sources agree to it, (2) it is congruent and coherent with respect to existing established knowledge, or (3) it possess a logical consistency of its own.

Since validity can never be fully attained the costs associated with achieving it can become astronomical. But the costs associated with faulty or misleading information are also large. Therefore, some degree of checking and testing and attention to detail is always in order.

Closely associated with the attribute of validity is that of *accuracy*. Accuracy assigns an error term to the information and provides some indication of how far from the true answer the reported information is likely to lie. If a clerk tells you that current inventory is 100 times plus or minus 10 (that is, its range is 90-110) he has provided you with an estimate of the error involved in accepting 100 as the true amount. The tighter the range, or in statistical terms, the smaller the "confidence interval" or standard deviation, the more accurate the data. Reporting the estimated error associated with an item of information always adds to its value because it permits the user to match the likely error to the needs of the problem at hand. Some users require only very crude "order of magnitude" estimates as long as they know that the true value likely lies in a contained range. We often call these "ball park estimates." Highly accurate information is generally costly to obtain; whereas decision relevant, "ball park estimates" may be adequate to achieve available benefits and much less costly to acquire.

The next two attributes—adequacy and scope—pertain more to the entire information system rather than to individual items of information.

ADEQUATE

An information system is adequate when it includes all of the information that is relevant to the user's purpose. Adequacy normally requires providing contextual information as well as key event information. Information on errors, exceptions, and assumptions generally adds to adequacy. Adequacy is achieved by fully understanding the network of relationships that ties items of information together and makes them an effective bundle within the users' environment. It further requires that users possess or have available the relevant portion of the network for any given situation.

A marketing executive planning a sales campaign for the Chicago market, for example, may need information on Chicago demographics, locations of dealers, financial information, employment and disposable income, the history of sales in the area and backgrounds of the people involved. When all of this diverse, relevant information is assembled and made available to the executives, then the system is adequate.

WIDE RANGING

Tunnel vision plagues managers. It also gets built into information systems.

An information system which is effective for the long term should be broad in scope and rich in insights and possibilities. It should be future oriented. Specifically, a wide ranging information system should provide information concerning the plausible options open to the organization and the possible opportunity costs or losses associated with each option. It should be creative and this means it should have aesthetic value as well as economic, scientific and political. As a result, this criteria is often in conflict with the others. A wide ranging information system may contain information initially considered to be irrelevant, unclear, unreliable and of questionable validity. It may be inadequate for current purposes. It may, however, provide the impetus for designers and users to create a new information system.

The observation that information attributes may be in conflict leads to one last point: trade-offs.

TRADE-OFFS AMONG ATTRIBUTES

Market researchers have an adage: "I can give you information which is accurate, rapid, or cheap. Pick *two*!" This kind of trade-off phenomena is present in all forms of information systems design. Information usually can be provided rapidly and at low cost if the user is willing to sacrifice accuracy. Accurate information frequently can be provided at low cost if it is collected and processed over a long period of time. And, quick and accurate information often can be provided if the designer is willing to devote enough resources to its collection, processing, and dissemination. The result is a "trade-off" triangle: Frequently designers must choose one of the sides of this triangle; or, in more complex situations, they must choose from among a host of multiple but incompatible attributes. What should guide this choice? In closing we round the conceptual circle again to say: It must be guided by purpose.

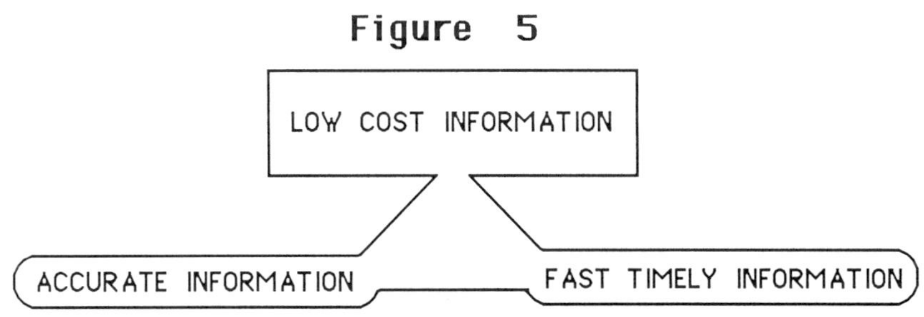

Figure 5

REFERENCES

Ackoff, Russell L. "Management Misinformation Systems"
Management Science. December 1967, p. 147-156.
Ackoff, Russell L. and Fred E. Emery. *On Purposeful Systems* Chicago: Alpine, 1972.

Churchman, C. West. *The System's Approach.* New York: Delacorate Press, 1967.

Churchman, C. West. *The System's Approach and Its Enemies* New York: Basic Books. 1979.

Marschak, Jacob. "Decision-making: Economic Aspects." *International Encyclopedia of the Social Sciences,* Vol. 4, Crowell Collier and Mac-Millan: New York, 1968, p. 42-55.

Marschak, Jacob. "Economics of Inquiring, Communicating, Deciding," *American Economic Review,* Vol. 58, No. 2, May 1968, p. 1-18.

Mason, Richard O. "Measuring Information Output: A Communications Approach," *Information and Management,* Vol. 1, 1978, pgs 219-234.

Mason, Richard O. "Measurement for Management Decision" Reading Mass: Addison-Wesley, 1981.

Savage, Leon and J. *The Foundation of Statistics* (Revised Edison) New York: 1972.

Singer, E.A. *Experience and Reflection* Philadelphia: University of Pennsylvania Press, 1959.

Wilensky, Harold L. *Organizational Intelligence* New York: Basic Books, 1967.

PART II

INFORMATION ARENAS AND APPLICATIONS:
EDUCATIONAL IMPLICATIONS

Robert M. Warner

ARCHIVES AND THE NEW INFORMATION
AGE: A RELUCTANT PARTNERSHIP

Information has become widely recognized as one of this nation's great resources. It should be. As our Society becomes more complex; as the data necessary for rational social and economic decisions increases and becomes more diverse, information becomes ever more important to us. At the same time, technological developments, particularly in the fields of automated data processing and telecommunications, are making information more easily stored and transmitted, more accessible, and more manipulable than ever before. As early as 1967, an analysis of the American economy by Porat and Rubin divided the economy into four sectors, of which information was one, and concluded that such a large proportion of the National resources were devoted to or dependent on information services that "the American economy is an information economy."[1] Five years later a report of the Congressional Office of Technology Assessment stated:

> The role of information in society is being changed under the influence of the new information technology. . .Over the next two decades [new] technology will likely change production processes and commercial goods, transportation and working patterns, the nature and content of education. . .and the way social values are formed and political decisions made. . . .[2]

As might be expected, this emphasis in information, powered by technological innovation, led directly to the developed within higher education of a new speciality: Information Science.

The clearest definition and explanation of Information Sciences that I know of is:

> Information Science is the study of how knowledge is communicated from the point of generation to the point of use—and all the intermediate steps of collecting, organizing, interpreting, storing, retrieving, disseminating, and transforming information.
>
> As a discipline, Information Science stresses the application of modern technologies to the handling of information.[3]

This is a broad definition indeed, a bit intimidating, but I believe it accurately reflects the central role of information in society.

The practitioners of this new specialty, as defined by a 1980 National Science Foundation study, are generalists (managers and educators), those with technical backgrounds in computer systems analysis and programming, and (the largest group) those trained in the principles of information—service—the use, interpretation, and dissemination of information.[4]

It is, I believe, this latter group that we are here to talk about today— the information service professionals. They are trained to acquire what users need; to arrange and process materials to achieve maximum conveniences and efficiencies. They are the bridge between information and the user, as well as the guide to the substantive content of the information.

Archivists stand squarely in the center of this group of information service professionals. Their professional jobs are to identify, arrange, describe, and make available the records in any form which they determine have sufficient historical or evidentiary value to warrent preservation as "permanent." They are truly a bridge between information and users, a guide to substantive content; they are information professionals.

As such, does the education traditionally required for archivists offer any clues to assist in exploring the topic of this conference: the intellectual foundations for informational professionals?

Archival education in the United States is a very recent development. Indeed, at the turn of the century, a distinguished historian and leader of the fight to establish a National Archives, compared the idea of training someone to become an archivist with preparing a person for being struck by lightning.[5] It was not until 1938 that the first formal course of instruction in archival management was offered at Columbia University's School of Library Science, which had been founded by Melville Dewey almost 50 years before. The Columbia Course, which was taught by a member of the National Archival staff, did not continue. But in the same year the newly founded Society of American Archivists formally addressed the problem of archival education by appointing a committee to establish training standards.

Under the direction of Samuel Flagg Bemis, the renouned diplomatic historian, the committee concluded that "historical scholars" equipped with "technical archival training" and whose work emphasized "American history and political science" should be the professional archivists of the future. The committee recommended that archivists receive the training required for a doctorate in American history (with a thesis requiring the use of a wide range of manuscript materials and public records) and that they complete a comprehensive course of the history of archives and archival practice which "might easily be grafted on the graduate instruction in American history in any first class American University."[6]

The Bemis report, although never formally accepted by the Society of American Archivists, established the philosophy of the archivist as a kind of historian, and thus set the tone for the profession for the next 30 years.

Two important examples of this view need to be mentioned here. First, when the National Archives was established exactly 50 years ago this year, the staff were mostly historians who had no technical preparation for their work. They adapted to the exigencies of their new profession and performed brilliantly in their work. This in turn undoubtedly led to the 1953 Federal government's Civil Service standards for the profession of archivist which required a college degree with two years of U.S. history and other courses in history, political science, economics, or public administration. The standards concluded with this sentence: "Experience as a librarian or analyst of nonhistorical files will not be considered qualifying" for the position of archivist.[7]

This latter point was a refutation of the argument that custodians of materials closely related to books should be trained in the same techniques as librarians. Archival methods, because of the nature and uniqueness of the material, had developed along very different lines. It was agreed, however, that knowledge of library methods could be a useful complement to an archivists skills, but would not meet his special needs. There was general agreement that a good general education plus a solid knowledge of American history and government were essential to the up-bringing of an archivist. The nature and scope of professional training could, presumably, be mastered on the job.

If archivists were not librarians, they were, despite their training, not really historians either. And, since their numbers were small, they were uncomfortable with being known only as archivists—a name that seemed to mean little to those who were not scholars or, in recent times, genealogists.

This lack of a clear identity haunts the profession to this day. There are numerous reasons and explanations for it, but one of the major factors that goes a long way to explaining the problem can be made clear by looking at the impact of archives on society, as opposed to that of libraries.

The immediate demand for the services of librarians at all levels of society, for all age groups, and in all places, caused that profession to establish standards and practices, to develop a high degree of proficiency, and to pass their accumulated knowledge along to the next generation of practitioners. Until recently archives, on the other hand, were little known or used by the general public, and the absence of external pressures helped make it possible for the profession to avoid self-analysis and definition.

The definitional process is now well under way. As early as 1976 the Society of American Archivists (SAA) issued its "Guidelines for Graduate Archival Education Programs."[8] This is particularly significant because there is no School of Archives in the United States (as there is in Germany or France, for example) and, as far as I know, there is no regular, full-time professor of archives in any educational institution in this country. To this day there is no professional accreditation of archival education programs in the United States, and no certification or licensing of practicing archivists.

The SAA "Guidelines" do stress both theoretical and practical education in the factors that make archives different from other professions —the emphasis on the uniqueness of the material held in archives and the necessity for its preservation, on the methods used to bring "intellectual control" over the enormous volume of material in archives, and the like.

They do not specifically require instruction in the application of modern technology to the handling of information.

Nevertheless, it is the existence of information handling technology that is not only determining the future of our profession, but is also drawing archivists, librarians, and other handlers of information together.

This convergence is not because the differences in the ways the professions do their jobs have been eliminated—they have not—but because the major problems (and opportunities) facing them are the same, and cooperation is mounting a common attack on them has developed. Only consider the common problems of libraries and archives, for example.

First and foremost among these is the intractable problem of all custodians of information—preservation. It is no secret that the holdings of libraries and archives are slowly disintegrating, what one recent writer referred to as the "quiet disaster." Modern paper, because of its acid content, decomposes in a few short years; photographs, because of the instability of their medium, fade, discolor, or buckle; microfilm can develop spots and render it unreadable; computer tape requires considerable attention if it is to be preserved. The list of horrors could go on and on, but the point should be clear; both libraries and archives are subject to the same problems. It is heartening to discover that the two professions recognize their community of interest and are beginning to share research information and data, to serve together on preservation committees and task forces and to join together to see that the American public is aware of the enormity of the preservation problem and the technological complexities involved.

Another area where archives and libraries are growing together is in the clientele they serve. Traditionally, as I mentioned before, archives tended to reflect their historical bias: they were, by and large, the creation of historians, and archivists were trained first as historians and only later as archivists. Librarians understood from the beginning that their clientele was all of society. But, in the past few decades, archivists have been learning this too. Today the largest single groups of users of the National Archives, other than the government itself, are not historians but rather genealogists. High school students, thanks in part to NARS created special materials to aid history instruction by using archives, are taking advantage of the resources of archives all over the nation. And, while we are hardly ready to begin mounting mobile archives depositories for school children, it seems clear that the lessons learned by libraries when serving a broad clientele are very appropriate for today's archives as well.

Archives and libraries are also drawing together because the types of materials they both hold are now often the same. At the National Archives, our holdings are mostly paper records, of course, but we also estimate that the collections include about 81 million feet of motion picture film, 5 million still photos, 1.6 million maps and architectural drawings, 72,000 sound recordings, 1,500 reels of machine readable records, and even about 100,000 museum objects (mostly in the presidential libraries). Other than the museum objects, can you think of any modern library which would not include all these categories of material?

But probably the major reason that archives and libraries have come together is the clear realization that both are fundamently concerned with the collection, storage, and subsequent availability of information.

For archivists, as information service professionals, this technology presents a dual challenge: not only must they master the technology in order to perform their day-to-day tasks, they must also master the handling of the records created by the technology. Lets look at this second problem first.

The full impact of the revolution created by information technology has not yet been felt. Word processors and desk top computers are becoming fixtures in every agency and office in the Federal government and elsewhere. Electronic mail is in its early stages, and technology is being developed for equipment that will revolutionize the office of the future, including not only improved word-processors but "intelligent" micrographics devices.[9] Such developments clearly will revolutionize the way in which records are created, managed, and used.

Paperless transmission and filing systems are a reality. The State Department does not make original paper copies of telegrams today. These documents are entered into computers, transmitted and received electronically, and stored on magnetic tape. The researchers and the archivist of the future will be forced to use the computer to obtain the data he needs.

These technological developments offer enormous opportunities for increasing the efficiency of record production, storage, and retrieval in modern offices. Yet they also create previously unknown risks for the alteration, misuse, and accidental or willfull destruction of valuable records. And records created by these means will be the archives of tomorrow.

How will archivists, as well as those to be trained as archivists, cope with this challenge and the opportunities the developments in information technology suggest?

First, we must increase our knowledge of information technology and develop our ability to handle records systems produced in this new form.

The National Archives' machine-readable archives division has been in operation for more than a decade. Its aggressive program for appraising the records in automated form and transferring these with continuing value to the Archives has forced changes in some of the ways we do things. Magnetic tape is fragile. Archivists therefore must appraise automated records and take custody of them without the usual archival delay of 20 to 30 years from creation to deposit. Archivists must also give particular attention to preservation of records in machine-readable form, making regular inspections and rewinding part of their routine program.

Some analysts have predicted that the "paperless" office eventually will become a reality. I am enough of a realist to believe that no office ever will be truly "paperless." Personal reminders, desk top calendars, diaries and other materials will continue to be written by hand on paper. And many of these personal materials will be the most significant sources of historical documentation. And what President of the United States will forego that beautifully embossed stationary to issue a proclamation in machine-readable form? Nonetheless, we must recognize that an increasing proportion and eventually the great majority of our nation's records will be recorded in automated form. And we will be giving more and more attention to these materials to ensure their long term accessibility.

We also are beginning to look at methods for converting records created in hard-copy to machine-readable form. Large-scale conversion is still years in the future. Noth only does the technology need to be fully developed and tested in archival applications—most importantly funds must be found to undertake such an ambitious project. Yet, even under the best circumstances out nation's archives can not and should not be completely reduced to non-paper form. Some documents—those having intrinsic value—must be retained in the original because of their significance or for particular information or evidence they contain.

As an obvious example, no one would consider throwing away the original Declaration of Independence or the Papers of the Continental Congress, even though these documents have been recorded and are safely preserved in non-paper format.

Nonetheless, archivists can and will use information technology to store and control their holdings and to make them more readily available to users. The Society of American Archivisit's National Information Systems Task Force is perhaps the most prominent example of archivists' efforts to harness information technology for archival goals.

In order to do their usual jobs, archivists are also increasingly experimenting with uses of automation for controlling records locations, for preparing descriptions, for indexing, and for other applications. I do not see the need for archivists of the future to become technological experts, but they must become adept at understanding new information technologies in order to control records produced in those technologies and to use those technologies for their own goals.

Finally—and I believe that this is critically important—Archivists must become more deeply involved in advising and assisting in the processes of records creation. At the National Archives we are implementing a new program to accomplish this—one intended to promote the creation of full records of Government activities and to ensure that the records are usable and protected. For want of better technology, we call this the "adequacy of documentation" program.

The goal of this program, put most directly, is to create a climate to make possible the best documentation of the organization, policies, and activities of the Government. This is a major change from most archival programs which affect records that have already been created used and are being prepared for disposition. Now we believe archivists must be involved at the time records are being created and record systems implemented. Why?

Because computers and other new record creation and and record keeping technologies are having a critical impact on the quality of records. Microfilming systems, word processors, and mini-computers all offer important advantages to managers. But each must be carefully reviewed from the archivist's point of view to assure that records of long-term value have protection against accidental destruction; that the physical form used has sufficient permanence for long-term use; that the records are not altered by unauthorized personnel; that future users will be able to find the information they need in the records.

These and other questions are the type that are being addressed by the NARS Documentation Standards staff and by the NARS initiated Inter-Agency Electronic Recordkeeping Task Group. You may have seen a recent front page story in the *New York Times* about this group and their concentration on the development of procedures for Federal employees to follow when using office automation systems.

One of their goals is to see that documentation and archival conerns are incorporated into the design of any automated information system, thus making the computer the "tool" of the archivist, while avoiding the cost—roughly 30 times more—to correct software deficiencies after a program is operational than to do so in the design stage.

All of this should make it clear that archives today and in the future will be directly affected by information technology. For the past two or three decades we have been living through what is commonly known as the information explosion. We are assaulted on all sides by messages—from print, electronics, satellites, data processing—until we have reached a kind of overload of our circuits, and no longer attempt to analyze or understand. But archivists, librarians, and other information professionals must understand and cope with this overload. This will require far more than a mastery of technology. It will mean development of theoretical bases to cope rationally with the problem.

Many thoughtful commentators on the American academic scene have concluded that the control and integration of the fragmented knowledge and information that characterizes out time will be the most important work of educators in the balance of this century. Marc Porat goes farther and states: "The difference between success and failure, survival and defeat, between being powerful and powerless, hinges more than ever before on understanding the value and importance of information— how to get it, organize it, protect it, use it, sell it, and not get overwhelmed by it."[10]

As we move toward deciding what instruction should be required for information professionals, recognizing their potential pivitol role in society, we must remember that a necessary component of information is human interaction. As Von Forester states:

> A library may store books, microfiches, documents, films, slides and catalogues, but it cannot store information. One can turn a library upside down: no information will come out. They only way one can obtain information from a library is to *look* at those books...documents, etc...Thus we see that information is created when a choice is made, but to be able to choose one must be free....[11]

Keeping this fact in mind, we still have the problem of defining what will be the intellectual foundations for the instruction needed to meet today's and tomorrow's changing information society. Out current frame of reference probably should not be destroyed, but few if any would argue that it should be kept intact.

One key component of the existing structure is the library profession. It developed, by the turn of the century, a clear identity that underwent modest and successful modifications during the next 50 years. This identity or self-definition has generally met the profession's needs. Now it has the problem of rethinking its definition and broadening it. I sense that many of the older library professionals feel uneasy—even threatened—by the prospect of change, as traditional librarians have difficulty in communicating with the new technologically based information science. Thus, there is a need to blend the old with the new and go beyond this amalgam to build new theoretical and practical foundations.

For archivists still seeking definition as a separate profession, my feeling is they should drop the search and view themselves in a larger context, with the potential to contribute to both the theory and practice of the information field. The unique archival contribution of the "life cycle of records" concept, developed in the National Archives, is easily, it seems to me, related to the broader theory of the information world; the archival idea of group description of materials can be useful to the control of the mass of information now being created. The overload of information and the seriousness of the problems this entailes came to the archival profession early. For example, all the records created by the U.S. Government between the founding of the country and 1930 were about 1/7 of those created between 1930 and 1952. In the Archives today, for example, we talk about 3-1/4 billion documents in our care. The computer oriented information manager, the part of the new information science whose identity is least clear, obviously has a role of growing importance in the future. But what it is I do not know. However, I do see a danger here of letting technology determine its nature. The answer will require more than technology; it must be based on sound theory and concern for human values and humanistic studies, which librarians and archivists now possess.

Thus in glimpsing at the future, always a dangerous role, I believe it will not be enough for the existing professions to stress their separateness and uniqueness. Instead they must move more to a growing together in a larger and yet undefined profession ecompassing librarian, archivists, information scientists, and other disciplines.

With the configuration it is obvious that the new profession will be interdisciplinary, including these groups already mentioned as well as management professionals, economists, all kinds of computer professionals, and even social and behavioral scientists. Recently I toured the Bell Laboratories to see a bit of that magnificant facility with its hundreds of scientists. I was especially impressed with their cadre of behavioral scientists doing research on the psychological and sociological impact of new forms of information and studying ways to explain and make acceptable new information delivery systems to various constituencies.

This visit also exemplified for me another component of the new profession a firm commitment to research. Such a commitment will, I believe, produce solutions to new information problems and, for the matter, some of the old ones like preservation as well. At the same time, research can be an important component in answering the question posed by this conference: "What are the intellectual foundations of the new information society?"

For now I believe that what educators must avoid is overreaction—remaking all education into "high tec" education. We must train students in how to learn—to use their minds to analyze and solve problems. In the future, most unthinking jobs will be done by machines. Computers (and indeed all technology) are tools. I agree with a Professor of Management who wrote recently:

> Computers are no substitute for sound basic educational preparation for life's many activities and roles. . . .Certainly, there should

be a place for a computer in every classroom, as there will be a computer in every aspect of life in the future. Still, the computer must be kept in its proper place.[12]

FOOTNOTES

1.   Cited in T. Wright, *A Discourse on Issues: An Exploratory Study of the Implications of Information Technology for UK Libraries and Information Work Manpower Planning,* Association of Special Libraries and Information Bureau, 1980, p. 26.

2.   Office of Technology Assessment, *Computer-Based National Information Systems: Technology and Public Policy Issues,* Government Printing Office, Washington, D.C., 1981, p. 48.

3.   Report of the Visiting Committee of the Baxter School of Library and Information Science to the University Commission on Information Sciences, unpublished, July 12, 1984, p. 4.

4.   Quoted in ibid.

5.   Julian P. Boyd, "Some Animadversions on Being Struck by Lightning," *Daedalus,* 86:49 (May 1955).

6.   Samuel Flagg Bemis, "The Training of Archivists in the United States," *American Archivist,* 2:160 (July 1939).

7.   United States Civil Service Commission, *Announcement No. 366,* issued March 31, 1953.

8.   "Guidelines for Graduate Archival Education Programs," *American Archivist,* 4:105-6. See also "Program Standard for Archives Education: The Practicum," *American Archivist* 44:420-22 (Summer 1980).

9.   Joseph W. Shepard, "The Future of Records Management," *Government Data Systems,* January/February 1982, p. 34.

10.   Quoted in the *Washington Post,* December 1, 1980.

11.   Quoted in Peter Lyman, "The Book and the Computer In An Age of 'Computer Literacy,'" *ACLS Newsletter,* 35:25-6 (Winter-Spring 1984).

12.   James O'Toole, "Getting Ready For the Next Industrial Revolution," *Washington Post,* October 7, 1984.

Forest Woody Horton, Jr.

EDUCATION FOR INFORMATION RESOURCES MANAGEMENT IN THE FEDERAL GOVERNMENT

Since the passage of the Paperwork Reduction Act of 1980 on December 11, 1980, progress toward putting in place educational machinery for training Federal level public officials in the theory and practice of Information Resources Management (IRM) has met with general success, but many problems still remain.

The United States Department of Agriculture's Graduate School has been a pioneer in developing a formal IRM curriculum, keeping in the forefront of new information and information technology economic, political and social issues, and training the first cadre of agency IRM officials who now number nearly 500.

This paper traces the evolution of these efforts and examines how they interrelate. Current as well as potential issues, problems and concerns are reviewed not just for the Federal sector, but for the private sector as well.

BACKGROUND

The Commission on Federal Paperwork was created by the Congress pursuant to Public Law 93-556 to investigate ways of reducing the paperwork and redtape burdens on the American public, indivudual citizens, businesses, institutions such as hospitals and colleges, lower levels of government, and others.[1] In committee hearings throughout the late sixties and early seventies, the Congress had been hearing with increasing vehemence the outcries of citizens and businesses who felt that government's intrusion into their lives via the routes of unnecessary forms, rules, regulations, reports, and record-keeping requirements had reached an unbearable point.

The Paperwork Commission first met in early 1975, reached a staff level of some 200 part-time and full-time positions including contractors and consultants, produced some 36 different reports, made some 770 recommendations, spent approximately $9 million dollars, and went out of business as a temporary commission in late 1977.

One of the most important of the 36 studies undertaken by the Commission was one that came to be known as the "Information Resources Management" or IRM study.[2] This study was one of five studies that were government-wide in scope and impact (others including the role of Congress itself as an instigator of paperwork, and the failure of the Federal, State and local levels of government to more closely synchronize and coordinate their paperwork requirements so as to minimize the duplicative and overlapping impact on respondents in the private sector).

The Commission found in its IRM study that an important cause of excessive paperwork is the Federal Government's treatment of information as a "free good" rather than as a "resource" like personal property, which should be managed. It found that there are many immediate and significant steps which could be taken to manage information resources, thereby minimizing paperwork that is excessive, redundant, unusable or unused.

The Commission's recommendations offered specific ways to allow Government to serve its citizens better with less, but more useful, information. The recommendations were premised on tried and tested principles, such as planning, accounting, budgeting and evaluating, which are used successfully in managing the government's other resources.

In its report, the Commission recognized that IRM embraces a multidisciplinary, if not interdisciplinary, view of information processing and data resource management. It therefore involves the assimilation and incorporation of theories, practical guides and tools used in many fields, including statistics, computer science, information science, cognitive psychology, the systems sciences, traditional paperwork control, records management, the management sciences, business administration, and others.

Traditionally, each of these fields has been viewed as being distinct insofar as its relationship to the management and control of paperwork and red tape is concerned. But the IRM function brings together these disciplines because their common denominator is better information collection, handling, dissemination and use. Common sense tells us that no single discipline, then, has a monopoly; each field has its own special and unique set of ideas and tools to offer. But they must be harnessed to pull together. The Commission found that as of the time of its investigations, each field was going its own way with the result that citizen was impacted with slightly different paperwork demands, each formatted in slightly different ways, perhaps required in different media (electronic, hard copy, microfilm), with different cut-off periods and data processing cycles, and so forth.

Clearly if each of these fields was to explore carefully how it should fit into the total IRM fabric, there must be a rethinking, a restructuring and a redesigning of Government's career, promotion, education and training programs to reflect this multidisciplinary character of IRM.

Three specific Commission recommendations addressed the career, education and training area:

Recommendation No. 11 (IRM Report, September 9, 1977)

The Director, OMB, should explore the feasibility of establishing a Joint Information Resources Management Program (JIRMP), patterned after the Joint Financial Management Improvement Program (JFMIP) as a multi-purpose vehicle around which efforts to revitalize, upgrade and modernize career, training and promotion opportunities and initiatives could be mobilized. This program would feature the issuance of a looseleaf notebook containing the latest information for information managers and technicians on new technology developments, good ideas and practices used by others to control paperwork, both good and bad experiences of practitioners, career opportunities for advancement and upgrading credentials in the many information fields, and so forth.

Recommendation No. 12

The Chairman, Civil Service Commission, should establish entry level classifications and examinations airmed at attracting outstanding candidates with degrees in business and public administration, liberal arts, library science, computer science, and other fields, to enter Government's Information Resources Management Program. Also, a new occupational classification series is needed, identifying specific responsibilities for the various kinds of information generalist and specialist positions required. Career and training opportunities, both on and off-the-job, should be developed to insure that lower and mid-level information managers, such as librarians, computer specialists, records officers and reports officers, can upgrade the quality and level of their technical and managerial skills in order to advance beyond mid-career levels where many are blocked.

Recommendation No. 13

The Director, OMB, the Chairman, Civil Service Commission, the Administrator of General Services, and other appropriate officials should undertake a joint project to consolidate, revise and update records management workshops and other courses on similar and related subjects to produce a single up-to-date series of workshops using the latest teaching methods, and incorporating the Information Resources Management principles and approaches the Commission is recommending.

Under a unique provision of Public Law 93-556 which established the Paperwork Commission, the Office of Management and Budget was required to report on the status of each of the 770 recommendations made by the Commission, to the Congress, every six months for the first two years following the submission of the Commission's final reports to the President of the Congress (meaning for the two year period September 1977 through September 1979). The Office of Personnel Management (OPM), which replaced the Civil Service Sommission, refused to establish a new occupational category for information management professionals called for by the Paperwork Commission, on the ground that it was much too early, in their view, for such a major new category to be established. Traditionally OPM takes decades to determine that a broad enough consensus exists to justify such a step.

Faced with this policy position from OPM, the individual Federal agencies were faced with a dilemma: if no formal occupational category existed for the new IRM positions established by the Paperwork Reduction Act of 1980 (which we"ll talk more about later), how would agencies find, train and enrich the career development of IRM job incumbents?

OPM had taken the position that any of these positions could be filled by virtually any kind of generalist incumbent, including program analysts, management analysts, administrative assistants, and so on. In short, their position was that the occupational category was a secondary, not primary consideration, and besides, they contended, it would take years for the specific functional authorities and responsibilities for each kind of IRM job to become well defined and crystallized.

It must be remembered that in the Federal Government's personnel systems, there are standards and guidelines for both the job itself (position classifications) and for the background and experience (both academic and on-the-job) of the incumbent/applicant (occupational classifications). The two may or may not match and often do not except in cases where long-standing and very rigorous accreditation and credentialing is required such as for physicians and lawyers. But there are exceptions even there.

In this vacuum of both statutory and policy leadership at the central agency management level (i.e. OMB, OPM, and GSA notably), the United States Department of Agriculture's Graduate School stepped in and established an IRM Curriculum Advisory Committee to begin work on a de facto IRM curriculum since the prospects of a de jure curriculum appeared so dim.

In a review of the early deliberations of this Committee, Montie points out that it first conducted a survey of universities to determine if any IRM programs existed and if the experience from these could be shared with the Graduate School.[3] Five schools were identified, but their programs were in such an early stage of development that they were not very valuable to the Committee.

After this survey, the Committee then decided to identify existing IRM type courses and construct conceptual models of IRM curricula to classify the courses and to identify areas not covered. It was determined that courses would need to be offered in both day and evening programs but since there were not sufficient daytime courses to utilize, the evening program would have to be relied upon as well. Four categories emerged: computer-related, graphic arts, laws and paralegal studies, and administration and management.

Several models for the IRM program were then suggested.

First, a Standards Model was proposed using a set of standards in four cluster areas: library/information sciences/archival knowledge and skills: ADP/telecommunications/photo-composition/word processing/micrograph ic knowledge and skills; management/human relations/interpersonal relations and communication/writing/listening/interviewing, and so on; and analytical/management analysis/statistical skills/other quantitative skills/economics/budgeting/accounting/and auditing knowledge and skills.

A second model called a "Skills Model" also emerged that embraced the following five areas: information handling technology, knowledge classification and organization, communications and human relations and management, analystical and problem-solving, and public administration including governance.

A third model proposed was a "Users Model" based on potential users of educational services: entry level professionals in an area such as librarianship or records management; knowledgeable professionals needing cross-training, dual-skilled persons, and top management (Senior Executive Service or SES).

Other models were proposed and during a period of a year or so there finally emerged a consensus on a curriculum framework. The Committee determined that three courses of action were essential:

First, that a full curriculum be developed as a framework for a formal certificate program (it must be remembered that the USDA Graduate School cannot offer degrees). The rational here as Montie points out was that the proposed courses were not directly related to existing jobs and, therefore, as independent courses would not attract sufficient numbers of students, an integrated curriculum would be needed. Conversely, there was enough similarity to existing courses to create an appearance of competition or redundancy (which, by the way, increasingly exists as technology courses and management courses proliferate in numbers to match the increasing proliferation of the technologies and their spin-offs as well).

Second, complete materials and recuit instructors for the curriculum, since the existing faculty and staff was not sufficiently knowledgeable about the new IRM concept and practice.

Third, update the list of existing courses to take into account horizontal bridges between them (e.g. the so-called Office-of-the-Future and Office Automation concepts, which cut across technology, organizational, functional and other boundaries).

By 1982 when the IRM Curriculum Certificate Program was finally put in place, some 31 different courses comprised the Federal IRM Curriculum; 30 Continuing Education Units (CEUs) was required. A year later, Jane S. Grymes of the United States Information Agency (USIA) became the Certificate's first recipient.[4]

At the present time, the existing Curriculum Committee has begun to review the list of courses to determine which ones might be dropped and/or transferred to the Computer Science, Library, or other curricula; which new ones might be added such as Decision Support Systems, Expert Systems, and Knowledge-Based Systems; and which ones might be subsumed with others or, conversely, split out from an existing course because the subject matter has become too complex and/or detailed (e.g information security, computer crime, copyright and the protection of intellectual properties).

Until now we have concentrated on the USDA Graduate School's initiatives because they have been pivotal. However, other Federal Agencies have also been experimenting with IRM curricula design and development. Among these is the National Defense University.

In October 1982 the National Defense University (NDU) convened a Select ("Blue") Ribbon Committee to review the "decision technology" area, including an evaluation of the curricula and academic program of the Department of Defense Computer Institute (DODCI).

One of the Blue Ribbon Committee's principal recommendations was that DODCI's curriculum be expanded to include courses focusing on the interface between the evolving military information and decision technologies of the 1980s and command/mission responsibilities such as C^3I. A related area of attention was to bring about more emphasis on the new information technologies such as microcomputers and executive work station applications.

The Select Committee drew on the work of the NDU Curriculum Advisory Committee that had been convened on September 1, 1981 to review the Armed Forces Staff College (AFSC) curriculum for modification reflecting revised educational emphases and new Presidential initiatives. Among the matters of priority interest to that study were:

—improvements in computer and telecommunications capabilities;
—using **ADP** to support war gaming;
—greater exchange of library resources horizontally and vertically among NDU components.

In early January of 1983, Dr. Carl Hammer, a noted computer authority and member of the Select Committee, recommended that NDU consider continuing research projects aimed at detailing just how the introduction of modern decision information management approaches, such as IRM, and the use of advanced information technologies within a DSS framework, could be more effectively integrated into the curricula of the NDU and its component colleges, institutes, centers, and other academic programs. A parallel outcome, Dr. Hammer suggested, would be the establishment of ongoing organic processes for the NDU to utilize in order to keep pace with the accelerating computer and information technology literacy demands on key military and civilian personnel within the Departments of State and Defense. He identified three key tasks in his research proposal:

1. improving the existing information and decision technology curricula;
2. developing computer literacy, sensitivity, and awareness among the faculty and students at NDU; and
3. structuring information and decision technologies within NDU.

At the present time NDU is moving aggressively to place the acquisition, use, management and control of information technology, including decision support and C^3I technology, squarely within an Information Resources Management (IRM) educational framework. An overall Education and Training Plan for Information Technology at NDU guides this effort, selling out its objectives, programs of instruction, major tasks, course listings, resources required and budgets, and other matters.

Before leaving the Department of Defense, it might also be pointed out that on March 8, 1983, Deputy DoD Secretary Paul Thayer signed a Memorandum for Members of the Defense Systems Acquisition Review Council re-emphasizing two important IRM principles: (1) data element standardization, and (2) the need to insure that information collected by DoD, or created by it, is used to serve some practical decision-making need.

Although the General Services Administration was perhaps most heavily involved of all the so-called central management agencies in re-organizing to prepare for IRM, it was a relative late-comer to establishing a formal IRM educational curriculum. But in its new Fiscal Year 1984 Catalog, the GSA Training Center has scheduled some 59 courses in major Federal population centers around the country, and training at additional locations can be arranged upon request.

In its announcement, the GSA Training Center states that it is "developing an integrated IRM curriculum that will encompass all phases of IRM-ADP, Telecommunications, and records management, for which GSA has government-wide responsibility." Presumably this means that information-related disciplines and programs for which GSA does not have responsibility will not be covered (e.g. statistics). An interesting course is called "managing records and information programs" and presents a strategy for managing records and information in the Federal Government using a total systems approach. It has four major components: program management, operations, analysis, and evaluation. The course is structured for new employees in the IRM field as well as others who want to learn a fresh approach.

Moving to the third Federal central management agency, the Office of Personal Management (OPM), the approach to IRM is anything but integrated. Information technology and information-related courses exist in a half dozen different curricula, and the threads are no where pulled together. Only two courses exist with a clear IRM framework. One is an information requirements analysis course that focuses on the needs assessment process—a very useful and virutally unique course in the total spectrum of extant Federal curricula (Code 23LE-C).[5]

The other is called "Information Resources Management: Analysis and Implementation (Code 23LG-C) and is squarely aimed at giving participants an overview of the Paperwork Reduction Act, the theory of IRM, the practice of IRM as it is being followed today in Federal agencies, and the various IRM tools such as the Information Collection Budget (ICB) and the Federal Information Locator System (FILS).

OPM subdivides its total program into "subject areas" which include administrative management, communications, computer courses for ADP specialists, computer courses for information users, executive and supervisory development, financial management, management sciences, office management, personal effectiveness, personnel management, planning and performance development, and special programs.

Information technology and information content related courses are strewn through more than half of these subject matter areas and are not synchronized so that students must pick and choose (mix and match) some combination of courses they feel they need.

One of the most important sources of education and training resources in the Washington D.C. area are the professional training organizations that continuously offer 1, 2 or 3 day workshops, seminars, tutorials, and other formats in various information technology and information content areas. Oftentimes the theme for such meetings is some "hot topic" of current prevailing interest to Federal employees, such as the privatisation of Federal information programs under OMB Circular A-76 ("contracting out"). Nearly two dozen such seminars and meetings on this one subject alone were offered in the Washington D.C. area in 1983 alone.

Occassionally private sector companies such as Informatics General Corporation or C.A.C.I. also offer IRM related seminars that are heavily marketed to Federal audiences, but by and large they have not been particularly successful.

A number of information professional societies are headquartered in the Washington, D.C. area and from time to time they, too, promote and market IRM related meetings of one kind or another. These include, for example, the Association for Federal Information Resources Management (AFFIRM), Associated Information Managers (AIM), the American Society for Information Science (ASIS), the Federal Library Committee, the Federal ADP Users Group (FADPUG) which has recently changed its name to Federal Computer Users Groups, and others.[7]

And finally, local Washington, D.C. area universities have mounted seminars, workshops, conferences and other kinds of meetings related to IRM or one of its component areas, including George Washington University, Catholic University, and the University of Maryland at College Park.

Evidence of regional and locally sponsored seminars outside of Washington is more difficult to compile, but nonetheless such meetings do infrequently take place with different groups such as the ones listed above often co-sponsoring the event.

FINDINGS AND CONCLUSIONS

1. Integrated IRM curricula in the Federal Government have been very slow to develop with the notable exception of the highly successful United States Department of Agriculture's Graduate School IRM Certificate Program.

2. There is some evidence that the USDA Graduate School's initiative may have had the effect of delaying or diverting the initiatives of the other central training agencies such as GSA and OPM, although the matter has never been formally investigated.

3. The absence of formal, detailed operational guidance from the Office of Management and Budget to the Federal agencies outlining exactly what is required of them in their IRM programs under the Paperwork Reduction Act of 1980 may be partly responsible for both the lack of initiative and the lack of specificity in IRM curricula thus far developed (i.e. their scope, interrelationships with other curricula such a Computer Science, determination of which courses that should be core and which elective, and so forth).

4. As more and more graduates of the USDA IRM program move from the "student" to the "alumni" category, their experiences in the "real world" of IRM in their agencies will be an important reservoir of experience to curriculum designers and curriculum enrichers who will be faced with the continuing task of upgrading and strengthening the early attempts at IRM curriculum design; these experiences should be systematically captured and collated.

5. The Federal Government, because of the Paperwork Reduction Act of 1980, is ambivalent over getting too far "out in front" of the private sector in developing educational machinery for IRM; experiences in installing and using IRM in the private sector (good case study materials) are still very hard to come by.

6. The Federal Government sees private and public universities in the middle of very significant "turf battles" over very fundamental questions of the roles of traditional academic disciplines in molding new Information Age curricula, and increasingly is adopting a "wait and see" attitude.

7. Some graduates of the very limited number of university IRM degree and certificate programs in the private sector are entering the Federal workforce, but their numbers are thus far minuscule and therefore their impact has been correspondingly low.

8. Most formal Federal training institutions such as the USDA seem to be almost totally preoccuped with computer literacy challenges, such that information literacy challenges are being deferred indefinitely. The consequences of this phenomenon have not been adequately studied. The "bottom line" seems to be "we have our hands completely full trying to keep up with the challenges of educating and training people on the proliferating new hardware and software products coming onto the market, such that we have time for virtually nothing else."

FIGURE 1-1

United States Department of Agriculture Graduate School Information Resources Management (IRM) Certificate Program

Required: 30 credits (CEUs)

Number	Title	Credits/CEUs
AIRAC 701	Paperwork Reduction Act of 1980 (P.L. 95-511)—Introduction	1.2
AIRAC 720	Luncheon Learning Seminars: An Overview of IRM	1.0
EMGMT 426	Introduction to Information Technology	3.0
	or	
AIRAC 715	Introduction to Information Technology	3.0
APUAP 855	Implementation of the FOIA and Privacy Act	1.2
ELAWS 335	The FOIA and the Privacy Act or	2.0
APAUP 856	Information Access Laws	1.8
ESTAT 101	Introductory Statistics 1 or	3.0
TSTAT 810	Statistical Sampling Techniques Workshop: Practical Applications for Government Management Analysts	2.4
EMGMT 252	Concepts of Office Technology	3.0
	or	
AIRAC 730	Word Processing and Office Automation	3.0
ACOMP 727	Getting the System You Want: A Users Guide to Project Management	0.8
TAUDT 875	Concepts and Approaches for Program Results Reviews	1.2
EMGMT 335	Introduction to the Federal Information Locator System (FILS) or	3.0
AIRAC 740	Introduction to the FILS	1.0
AIRAC 710	Advanced Seminar on Information Management in Public Administration	3.2
EMGMT 340	Management Information Systems or	3.0
ACOMP 735	Management Information Systems	1.8

FIGURE 1-2

**United States Department of Agriculture Graduate School
Information Resources Management (IRM) Certificate Program**

Number	Title	Credits/CEUs
TAUDT 720	Effective Government Auditing	3.0
	or	
TAUDT 730	Governmental Auditing—An Overview	
	for Investigators	1.8
EMGMT 310	Advanced Records Management	2.0
EGART 245	Computer Forms Design and Production*	2.0
ACOMP 370	Teleprocessing and Data Communications	2.4
	or	
ECOMP 224	Teleprocessing and Data Communication	
	Systems	4.0
TCOMP 859	Introduction to ADP Auditing	3.0
	or	
ECOMP 582	Computer Security and Privacy	3.0
ESTAT 401	Introduction to Statistical Software	4.0
ACOMP 910	Telecommunications: An Introductory	
	Overview for Managers	1.2
ELIBT 400	Advanced Strategies for Online Biblio-	
	graphic Searching	3.0
AIRAC 720	Luncheon Learning Seminars:	
	An Overview of IRM	1.0
APAUP 856	Information Access Laws	1.8

* to be transferred to Computer Science Curriculum

BIBLIOGRAPHY

1. Final Summary Report, A Report of the Commission on Federal Paperwork, October 3, 1977, Government Printing Office, Y 3.P 19:1/977 (1977 248-092).
2. Information Resources Management, A Report of the Commission on Federal Paperwork, September 9, 1977, Government Printing Office, 052-003-00464-0.
3. Montie, Irene C., Developing an Information Resources Management Curriculum, Bulletin of the American Society for Information Science, June 1983, V9 N5, pp. 12-17.
4. Information Resources Management, 1984 Course Module, USDA Graduate School, 600 Maryland Avenue, S.W., Room 106, Washington, D.C. 20024.
5. FY 1985 Training and Developing Services Catalog, Office of Personnel Management, WD-17, June 1984, available from OPM or Government Printing Office (447-410/1984).
6. IRM—The Information Management Newsletter, V3 N2 and V3 N1, Information Management Press, P. O. Box 19166, Washington, D.C. 20036.
7. Information Management in Public Administration, F. W. Horton, Jr. and D. A. Marchand, Information Resources Press, Arlington, Va. 22209 (1700 North Moore Street).
8. The GSA Training Center Catalog and Schedule, Fiscal Year 1984, GSA Training Center, P. O. Box 15608, Arlington, VA 22215-0608.

Rena L. Fugate

RECORDS MANAGEMENT:
A GLOBAL PERSPECTIVE TO INFORMATION

INTRODUCTION

Records management involves the same underlying theories and concepts of library and information management—understanding of user information needs, the storage of information and effective retrieval. There are more similarities than differences between records management and library science, with the differences surfacing primarily in the application areas. A well thought out, applied records management program can enhance any area where information is used.

Records management includes the data gathering, analysis, planning, and organizing necessary for managing information throughout an organization. Concepts of records management can be applied to all types of business, government, educational institutions, non-profit organizations, and to personal files. Since records management is applicable to many areas the term organization will be used generically to refer to them all.

This paper will highlight most of the processes that define records management to insure a global perspective is presented and to emphasize the interrelationships between the processes such that very few decisions can be made which will not affect the ones preceding or following.

Records management, like librianianship, is facing change brought about by technology. In addition to discussing records management processes, this paper will identify positions available to the "traditional" records manager, and those growing out of the changes. Since markets for many of the new positions are in the beginning stages of development, this paper will also address the role, as well as the responsibility, for the educator, the school and the alumni in promoting the information professional for these positions.

RECORDS MANAGEMENT

A properly applied Records management program will provide an organization with the ability to:

1) be able to retrieve needed information in an efficient and effective manner.
2) eliminate the purchase of surplus equipment and supplies, including file cabinets, file folders, computers and software.
3) provide the organization with the ability to meet retention requirements, both legal and organization related.
4) eliminate the chances of retaining to much information which in the case of litigation could result in the need to produce much more evidence than is necessary.

Professor Mark Langemo, Professor at South Dakota University, generated a list of several benefits which can result from the implementation of a records management program. These include: 1) increased top management efficiency and success because information is available to support decision making; 2) increased ability to maintain the competitive edge; 3) an improved "profit picture" because administrative back office support systems are streamlined and wasted time and effort are reduced; and 4) a positive image of the organization.[1]

Maedke sets forth the totality of records management as the "application of systematic and scientific control to the recorded information that is required in the operation of an organization's business. Such control is exercised over the creation, distribution, utilization, retention, storage, retrieval, protection, preservation, and final disposition of all types of records within an organization."[2]

The definition of records is broad and includes data or information contained in/on any medium, e.g. a piece of paper, a diskette, electronic impulses recorded on a diskette, map, photographs, or film.

The Need for Records Management

"America has a problem. . . . Somewhere in the offices of this land of ours 21 trillion pages of paper are stored away and businesses chun out roughly 600 million pages of computer printouts, 235 million photocopies and 76 million letters daily."[3] The increasing amounts of paper, the numbers of clerical personnel required to handle the paper and the resulting labor cost are concerns of most organizations.

Of greater importance, is the concern over the ability to retrieve information when needed since records provide the information organizations need to make decisions and solve problems. "The management of records is actually the management of information. Information is valuable to the operation of any organization, and the specialty of records management is the efficient direction and protection of this information during its useful life to the firm."[4]

Almost all of the costs related to improved records management processes are intangible and difficult to measure. One of the most tangible of all is the one most important to an organization, that of being able to find the information when needed, since the cost of a "dead" deal can be substantial.

The scope of records management program will be governed by the needs of the users and by the size and type of the organization. By design the programs performs service, advisory and control functions. The service function, through retrieval systems and properly trained personnel, provides management with the information necessary for problem solving and decision making. The advisory function involves finding solutions for operating problems that develop during records creation, active and inactive maintenance and records disposition. The control function is part of each process where establishment of standards and guidelines are necessary to insure continuity of the service and advisory functions.

CREATION PROCESS

One of the increasingly important processes to control is creation. As mentioned above, significant amounts of paper have been created. The introduction of the word processor, computers and convenience copiers have contributed to this creation.

Correspondence ranks second to forms in business records volume. The average cost of creating a business letter as calculated in 1982 by Dartnell Institute was $10 and if new technology is taken into account, the cost may be significantly higher. Control of the creation process would: 1) limit the creation of communications to essential requirements; 2) insure that all such records are of the highest quality; and 3) expedite the preparation and processing of communications.

An objective of a correspondence management program is to improve the understandability of correspondence so that its purpose is met. Robert Gunning, an authority on the measurement of readability and author of *How to take the Fog Out of Writing,* found that most readability could be kept at or below the eleventh grade. As a method of calculating readability, he developed the Fog Index which is based on the number of words in a sentence and the number of syllables per word. If the result of this calculation is greater than 12, Gunning believes an author is in danger of being ignored or misunderstood.[5]

The user or creator has a significant role in meeting the objectives of the creation process. For example, the user must assign a title or subject to each record as it is created through the use of the classification system; determine the retention value of the record, i.e., 90 days, one year, or vital; and determine number of copies and provide the time frame for distribution.

Another area of concern in an organization is that of handling forms. Christian shows that 79% of the cost breakdown of a form is spent on usage, employee labor, machine cost and space costs, 11% on filing and maintenance, 5% on printing costs, 2% on storage and distribution and 3% on purchasing, receiving and accounting.[6]

Thorough analysis of both the users and the organization need is necessary to insure that proper decisions are made relating to ongoing requirements. For example, if a form is to be retained for a period of 15 to 20 years, then carbonless paper may not meet the need since the writing on carbonless paper has been known to fade after several years. The need to follow a form through from creation to disposition is reinforced when one can see the impact of a decision made today in the long term life of a form.

DISTRIBUTION PROCESS

The handling of information, both incoming and outgoing, can have an impact on the effectiveness and efficiencies of the organization. The mail room, for example, is a cost center which has been a control point in the organization for receiving and sending information. The role of the mail room appears to be changing with the introduction of many of the technologies. Distribution and delivery of information can now occur via computer, facsimile, or telecommunications. The mail room may soon be only a clearinghouse for third and fourth class mail.

RETRIEVAL PROCESS

Organizations and individuals retain information because there is perceived future value in the information. The ability to retrieve is then a primary process to develop and control. Initial data gathering for development of the classification system(s) will be the completion of a records and fill equipment inventory. These inventories also provide information about the what and who of the organization, as well as indicating the kinds of records being held by each person, department, division and company, how old they are, what labels people attach to them, and where and how they are stored.

The file equipment inventory will show who has the equipment and its utilization. Statistics taken from file equipment inventories have shown that one drawer in four contains active records requiring access, one drawer will contain inactive records which could be sent to storage, and two of the four will be empty, contain supplies, or other nonrecord materials. The implementation of a system which provides control over file equipment can result in savings to an organization through cost avoidance by reducing the possibility of purchasing new equipment. It will also show where, with proper utilization floor space can be reclaimed and used for people instead of paper.

Analysis of the file inventory, combined with interviews of users will provide information required to develop an effective classification system. A classification system provides the organization necessary to insure that information such as correspondence, forms, reports, and memoranda can be retrieved. Two basic classification systems exist: alphabetic and numeric. Alphabetic systems are considered to be direct access systems, allowing people to go directly to the information, while a numeric system is indirect requiring a person to look up the number to find the alpha relationship.

Both systems will have a place in an organization. Alpha systems are most applicable to subject files, geographic files, and people files. Numeric systems are used in many accounting applications, medical/patient records and for very, very large volumes of records.

A uniform subject classification system based on the specialized needs of the organization will result in ease of filing and retrieval. Relationships between various subject areas are developed with the result that fewer files are created and less equipment is necessary. Retrieval is timely since the user and the support personnel use the same terminology about a subject; and person dependent systems are eliminated.

STORAGE PROCESS

Active Records—Equipment and Supplies

Frost & Sullivan, in a 1983 study, found that "Office filing equipment to handle paper and computer paper records will rise 51%. . . hitting $2.6 billion in 1987 (up from $1.7 billion in 1982.)"[7] Statistics show that 56% of the file equipment in an office is occupied by files, that over 40% of file space is in excess of present need, that 85% of records filed are never looked at again, that 40% to 50% of present filed materials could be destroyed or moved to low cost storage and that 90% of the records sent to storage are never seen again.

The selection and purchase of file equipment and supplies for active records are dependent on user needs, the classification system, space availability, accessibility and budget restrictions. Analysis of the foregoing and the correct choice of file equipment will save the organization time and money.

Changes made in equipment will affect supplies, retrieval and floor space. For example, legal size file equipment and supplies cost an organization 30% more than letter size. ARMA, Association of Records Managers & Administrators, challenged the federal court system to change their requirements from legal to letter size paper. A project titled "Eliminate Legal Files" or "ELF" was born on January 1, 1983 the federal courts changed their requirements and only letter sized documents were acceptable. A primary objective in introducing the change was to reduce costs but the decision affected current activity, because existing forms, procedures and word processing formats were set to create legal sized documents. Over time, an organization will reduce the need for legal size file equipment, and thus its cost.

RETENTION PROCESS

Much of records and information management is linked to the application of common sense, and this is especially true to the development of a retention schedule. A retention schedule is an ongoing process, because, due to changing organization needs the schedule will require review and updating.

A retention schedule provides documentation about the decisions an organization makes related to retaining and disposing of records. Approximately 10% of the records held by an organization are governed by law and legal regulations. The percentage may be higher, if the organization is highly regulated, but using the 10% figure, most records, or 90%, are retained to meet administrative, operational or historical needs.

The records manager does not make decisions about the length of time to retain records. Rather, the records manager can do the research to locate specific citations for records retained to meet legal requirements and can assist in developing suggested periods for operational and administrative requirements. The final determination of the retention periods will be made most often by a committee which includes representatives of tax, audit, finance, and legal departments as well as the records manager. This committee would also approve the final destruction of all scheduled records.

Searching the literature for information on retention schedules generates a fair amount of material, almost all of its useless. A key to a useful schedule is the applicability to the records of the specific organization.

The uniform classification system mentioned above provides the standardization needed for titling and building a useful retention schedule. Unfortunately, the published schedules are not easily related to the records inventory. In evaluating any schedule and the time periods suggested, it is important to know the background of the publisher. A schedule produced by a company that sells shredders may be considered different from one by a company who is in the records storage business.

A common fallacy in discussing retention requirements occurs when Statutes of Limitations are believed to establish the critera for retention. Statutes of Limitations specify the time after which legal rights cannot be enforced by civil action in court. These statutes do not specifically require the keeping of records and should not be allowed to confuse setting retention periods.

Inactive Records

Once information is no longer required for the everyday business at hand, but must be retained for a period of time, i.e., 12 months to 999 months, relocating to an off site storage facility can be considered. Major considerations when evaluating an off site storage facility are those of retrievability and security.

Depending on organizational needs, inactive records are generally stored in either a warehouse belonging to the organization or a commercial off site storage facility. In the latter, a separate organization owns and operates the facility providing the necessary services related to retrieval and handling. In the warehouse, the responsibility for operating remains with the organization. The warehouse must be equipped with proper shelving, safety and security procedures established and personnel trained.

The storage box is the basic supply required for storing records. The best box for storage is the cubic foot box measuring 12" x 15" x 10.5", which is tested to hold up to 200 pounds. This box will hold letter and legal files and a full box will weigh on average 40 punds. Transfer cases are a problem for storage. Although the size looks fine, the boxes are too heavy to life since they weigh about 80 pounds. These cases cost more to purchase and cost more to store. The need to consider the impact of each decision relating to records management is reinforced by this simple example of the problems that can occur when inadequate boxes are used.

PROTECTION PROCESS

Vital Records

Vital records are those which the organization needs if there is a fire in the building and everything is destroyed. Approximately 2%-4% of a company's records will be considered vital records. Several classifications of vital records exist, but the classification of greatest concern is for those records determined to be essential to the organization and which cannot be recreated.

Most large data processing environments have backup systems which eliminate the possibility of losing more than one days work. Unfortunately, most organizations do not pay the same amount of attention to those records retained on paper or other media. An organization which cannot track its accounts receivable may face serious consequences.

Vital records in an organization will be defined by the users, but proper safeguarding will fall to the records and information management personnel. Vital records can be either active or inactive. Active records are more problematic to secure since they must be available to the users for ready reference. Inactive records with lower retrieval can generally be stored and secured more easily off site.

PRESERVATION PROCESS

Records personnel must maintain an awareness of the role of the historical information in the organization and take care to insure that it is properly handled. Historical records and information will generally require handling by those specially trained in archival management.

TECHNOLOGY AND RECORDS MANAGEMENT

To effectively utilize technology, integration is projected as essential. John Connell in *Business Week,* writes that two developments will revolutionize the world of information technology, first, changes of traditional definitions of specific technologies and the blurring of distinctions among them; and second, the interconnection of previously separate technologies through integrated telecommunications networks. These two developments will eventually lead us to the integrated network.

Technology is changing the way we create, distribute, utilize, store, retrieve and protect information; but, the same concerns that were important in a paper based system are as important, with the new technologis. We still have to understand the user requirements, the need to retrieve being a key element in any system, and standards and guidelines must be in place or we face the loss of significant amounts of information.

CAREER OPPORTUNITIES

Records management programs vary in structure and size according to the organization and no two programs are the same. A successful records management program requires the assistance and cooperation of all personnel in an organization and commitment from executive management. Control of the records management program is generally assigned to one department and the trained staff. "Management should now employ the services of a records manager, for this is the only person qualified to analyze the present situation and chart a course of action for the records management program. It is important to remember that in most cases records management problems have developed and evolved over a long period of time. The temptation to utilize a quick-fix solution will be great."[8]

A Records Management department in an organization, might include the following positions: Director, Records Center Supervisor, Micrographic Services Supervisor, Records Management Coordinator, Records Management Analysts, Reports Manager, and Forms Manager. Larger organizations will require this level of staffing, while smaller organizations may have a records manager who is responsible for all of the processes.

In most organizations, information resources are managed as individual entities related to the form in which the information is obtained

   —the librarian manages the library of externally generated information
   —the records manager manages the internally generated information
   —the data processing manager manages the information contained
     on disk and tape.

The concept of information resource management recognizes the dispersion of responsibility and calls for an integration of information content in whatever form—either text or numeric and from whatever source—internal or external. This concept shifts the emphasis away from the format or delivery system to the content.

Where does the information resource manager come from. Robert Diamond, publisher of IRM, wrote "Information . . . managers can emerge from any number of functions, including records management, data processing management, financial management, and general management. . . . It is not so much where the manager comes from, but where he or she is going. The records manager is perhaps the strongest contender for the job, as his role has already placed him in a position of being an information resource for all segments of the organization."[9]

"People in records management have to decide what their role will be—a diminished one as activities change, or an increased one as they apply proven principles and practices. . . ."[10] Records managers who remain alert to changes within organizations will see developing opportunities for application of their skills. Information management positions will not necessarily mean that one must know how to program in six languages, but it does mean that there is some understanding of the new technologies, the effect each can and will have on the dissemination and retrieval of information and how technology will meet the needs of the organization.

One important role for information managers to develop and promote is that of gatekeeper. In that regard, we must remain cognizant of the need to guard against "junk" information. "Gradually the notion is sinking in that somebody somewhere in today's business organization needs to control the flow and sheer tonnage of all the information that does "get through," not just by processing it better, but by judging its likely value to the people who receive it. If some of it is useless, don't process it. If it's not worth distributing widely, distribute it selectively. That's gatekeeping."[11]

The need for a gatekeeper is reinforced since we have the capability to create, produce and make information available faster and faster. Unless there is some way to "gatekeep," the sophistication of the capability will be lost. Naisbitt, gives an example in his book, *Megatrends*,[12] about the numbers of scientific studies that are produced and made available; instead of helping, some scientists say they can often do the experiments faster than try to wade through all related information.

There is considerable blurring in today's office of who might be best prepared to manage the office of the future. Very often data processing people are thought to be better prepared for the responsibilities since so much of what is developing is computer oriented. Often though, data processing people are narrowly focused and do not necessarily related either to the information or the people who have need for the information.

"Nearly 20 million new jobs were created in the 1970s, 90% of them in the information/knowledge/service sector."[13] The need for personnel trained and exposed to information management theory continues, and, emerging information managers have the opportunity to take the initiative and lay out the road. The value of the information manager will be based upon perceptions that only the information manager can create. The information manager of the 1980s will be an individual who is capable of integrating and synthesizing information based upon an understanding of the users role and responsibility within the organization.

ROLE FOR THE EDUCATOR,
SCHOOL AND ALUMNI

"A decade-long shift from institutional help to self help has brought about a reemergence of the traditional American value of self-reliance.[14] This philosophy is being carried over into the education institutions as indicated in a recent article in *Business Week*[15] discussing university strategic planning. The article noted that Carnegie-Mellon is engaged in strategic planning that focuses on the school's customers—its students. There is discussion and concern over the role of the institution in educating as compared to training. This author perceives a need to strike a balance between education and application of knowledge. Many students upon graduating look to be employed in a reasonably well compensated position. In order to attract students to a school, their needs must be understood and met, but not necessarily to the detriment of the educational program.

There has been a perception that education follows business in providing a work force. In the case of information management, some information management programs are leading by graduating students who are prepared for information management positions before the need has been clearly recognized by the organizations. The program in information management developed by Dean Roger Greer at USC provides students with a choice for application which may be a career in a library or in the new developing positions of information managers. The benefit of this approach is that students have greater career opportunity for positions just now beginning to be recognized.

Defining the student needs is parallel to those of a business doing market research. Knowing what the jobs are, where the jobs are, educational requirements and application experience needed, will result in the development of a relevant curriculum which can be marketed and sold to the students. Researching the what and where of job availability can be promoted as a responsibility of faculty and alumni. These two groups can play an important role in developing networks between the school and the potential employers. The responsibility of the educator, institution and alumni then, is to go forth and assist in developing the market for the students which, in turn, will market the school.

CONCLUSION

Records management involves the application of all the principles that underlie an information focused curriculum. The same theories drawn from the social science disciplines that help explain information use behavior, knowledge creation and recording, dissemination and diffusion of information, etc. can be drawn upon by the records management. The records manager must understand both the organization and the organizing of its information. The store of concepts drawn from systems and contingency theory, organization and networking theory and other relevant theories, provides the broad base upon which specific training in records management techniques rests. This conceptualization of an information studies education allows freedom to choose from a variety of growing career fields.

Career opportunities are on the increase for those with information education and training. Understanding records management, where it fits in the organization, and the interrelated processes of information creation, use, retrieval and storage provide a global perspective to information mangement, as well as unlimited application opportunity.

NOTES

1.   Mark Langemo, "Selling Records Management," handout at ARMA seminar (Washington, D.C., 1979).

2.   Wilmer O. Maedke, Mary F. Robek, and Gerald F. Brown, *Information and Records Management* (Encino, Ca: Glencoe Press, 1981), 5.

3.   Louis E. Washington, "Reaping the Rewards of Sound Records Management," *S.A.M. Advanced Management Journal* (New York: Society of the Advancement of Management, Summer 1983): 45-52.

4.   Ibid., 48.

5.   Maedke, *Information and Records Management,* 218.

6.   C.W. Christian, "Four Major Functions of a Forms-Management System," *The Office,* July 1983, 77.

7.   "Still in the files," *Office Administration and Automation,* July 1983, 22.

8.   Washington, "Reaping the Rewards," 50.

9.   Robert Diamon, "Editorial," *Information and Records Management,* February 1982, 5.

10.   "The Changing World of the Information Manager." *Information and Records Management,* May 1980, 12.

11.   Walter A. Klimschood, "Who Will be the Gatekeepers of the Information Stockyard?" *Office Administration and Automation,* August, 1983, 12.

12.   John Naisbitt, *Megatrends,* (New York: Wanrer Books, 1982), 24.

13.   Melanie Mitzner, "Drowning in Data? Help is on the Way!", *Computer Decisions,* June 1984, 67.

14.   Naisbitt, *Megatrends,* 2.

15.   "How Academia is Taking a Lesson from Business," *Business Week,* August 27, 1984, 58.

BIBLIOGRAPHY

Aschner, Katherine, ed. *Taking Control of Your Office Records,* White Plains, New York: Knowledge Industry Publications, 1983.

Association of Information and Records Management. *Bibliography on Records Management.* Prairie Village, Kansas, 1980.

Diamond, Susan Z. *Records Management: A Practical Guide.* New Yok: *Amacom,* 1983.

"Document Retention and Destruction: Practical, Legal and Ethical Considerations." *Notre Dame Lawyer,* 56 October 1980.

Grossman, Lee. *Fat Paper.* New York: McGraw-Hill, Inc. 1976.

Knox, Frank M. *The Knox Standard Guide to Design and Control of Business Forms.* New York: McGraw-Hill, Inc. 1965.

Lybarger, Phyllis M. *Records Retention Scheduling.* Prairie Village, Kansas: *ARMA,* Technical Report No. 1, 1980.

Maeke, Wilmer O.; Mary F. Robek; Gerald F. Brown. *Information and Records Management.* 2nd ed. Beverly Hills, CA: Glencoe Press, 1974.

Mitchell, William E. *Records Retention.* Evansville, Indiana: Ellsworth Publishing Co., 1976, revised.

Naisbitt, John. *Megatrends.* New York: Warner Books, 1982.

Osteen, Carl E. *Forms Analysis: A Management Tool for Design and Control.* Stamford, Conn: Office Publications, Inc., 1969.

Ricks, Betty R. and Gow, Kay F. *Information Resource Management.* Cincinnati, Ohio: South-Western Publishing Co., 1984.

Records Retention Timetable. New York: Electronic Wastebasket Corp. latest edition.

The Retention Book: Retention and Preservation of Records with Destruction Schedules. 11th edition. Chicago, Illinois: Records Control, Inc. 1984.

Waegemann, C. Peter. *Handbook of Records Storage and Space Management.* Westport, Conn.: Greenwood Press, 1983.

PART III

CONCEPTS AND INFORMATION

Gordon B. Davis

INFORMATION SYSTEMS AS AN
ACADEMIC DISCIPLINE*

Information Systems (or Management Information Systems) is an area of academic study usually located administratively within schools of management or business administration. However, it may be located within other academic homes such as computer science. Within a school of administration, information systems may be independent or be part of another department such as accounting or management sciences.

This paper explores the evolution of information systems as a new area of academic study and research. In the context of this exploration, it should be noted that the school of management academic host for information systems is itself fairly young as an academic unit. For example, the Harvard Business School celebrated its 75th anniversary in 1983. The fields of study within business are also young as academic disciplines (except perhaps economics). As an illustration, the *Accounting Review,* the journal that represents the study of accounting as an academic discipline, is only 55 years old.

Information systems is the newest of the new. It is going through the ill-defined process by which a new field becomes a legitimate academic discipline. The process began in the mid-60s, so there is less than 20 years of development, and the process is not yet completed. The description in

* This paper is a modification and extension of the Keynote Address by the author at ISECON83, the Information Systems Education Conference, Chicago, 1983, sponsored by DPMA, and a paper delivered at the Information Systems Section at the ASAC Conference 1983, University of British Columbia.

the paper is that of a participant because I have been part of the development, and I will often refer to things I have done or written because they are the most ready evidence for explaining what I perceive has happened and is happening.

Information systems is challenging because it is at the interface of many fields and includes many processes and concepts, each of which is interesting in itself. The boundaries of the academic field are still very fluid, and so people in the field continue to have the excitement of intellectual exploration within the constraints of traditional methods and traditional boundaries

ACADEMIC DISCIPLINE VERSUS VOCATIONAL TRAINING

It is useful to define "academic discipline" and to distinguish it from courses of study that are generally labelled "vocational." Vocational courses of study are generally though of as being oriented to the specific requirements and job skills for the immediate, proximate job position. The vocational curriculum is therefore closely matched to current practice. An academic discipline has a longer-term orientation. The course content has a heavy emphasis on underlying principles and concepts for understanding the field and for formulating new answers as the field changes. The content of courses includes material related to current practice, but there is more emphasis on directions and underlying phenomena. There is a feeling that much of specific current practice is best taught on the job.

In an acadmic discipline, faculty members are evaluated on their command of underlying principles, concepts, and phenomena; this is most frequently demonstrated be research and publications. Both the vocational and the academic discipline approach are valuable and have their place in our educational system. However, within the context of the university, a field will never flourish unless it is an academic discipline.

SOME INDICATORS OF CURRENT ACADEMIC STATUS

There are some facts and observations about the information systems field and the faculty who staff it.

**Names Titles, and Acadmic Home for
Information Systems**

The field we are addressing has a number of different academic titles.
There is no agreement on what a department or area should be called.
I will use the term "information systems," but other titles have significant use. In a 1979 survey of 124 programs by Nunamaker, et at. (1981),
the titles of programs were as follows:

Number	Name
27	Management Information Systems
18	Information Systems
5	Business Information Systems
4	Computer Information Science
4	Business Data Processing
3	Computer Information Systems
3	Information Processing
3	Information Systems Analysis and Design
3	Information Science
9	Names occuring twice
18	Names occuring once

The location of the information systems academic area within the university is generally in the school of business administration. This is demonstrated by the 87 schools meeting criteria for an information systems
program that were identified in the Nunamaker, et al., survey.

	Bachelor's	Master's	Total	Percent
Business or Management College	42	25	67	77
Computer Science or Engineering	11	9	20	23

The Information Systems Faculty

I estimate that there are over 100 faculty members in North America
who would classify themselves as information systems faculty. These

estimates are based on the 504 faculty from 133 schools in the 1983 MISRC/McGraw Hill Directory of MIS faculty. Because it is the first directory of its kind, there are faculty who did not get listed and a few schools that are not included. The directory will be updated in early 1985 (and may be extended to other countries). Note that the faculty are in the directory because they classified themselves as information systems professors.

There are an average of 3.7 faculty members per school. In general, I feel that it requires at least four faculty to cover the subject matter and establish areas of competence. The distribution among schools for faculty listed in the directory is instructive:

Number of Faculty at the School	Number of Schools
1	44
2	17
3	11
4	18
5	9
6	12
7	6
8	5
9	6
10 or more	5

Note that 72 of 133 schools in the directory have 3 or less faculty. Even allowing for faculty not listed, almost half of the schools lack a critical mass of information systems faculty.

The Academic Degrees for Information Systems Faculty

There are 36 North American universities (three of them in Canada) that offer a doctorate in information systems (as listed in MIS Interrupt). About 30 to 40 doctoral degrees are awarded each year in information systems with about 70 percent taking academic positions. However, there are 100 to 150 unfilled academic positions for information systems faculty.

A characteristic of the population of information system faculty is that well over half of them did not get their primary degree in information systems. Their doctorates are in related fields, and they may have little formal study in the field. They faculty is nonhomgeneous in background, and this adds variety to the research and approaches taken; on the other hand, this causes the field to appear to be so diverse as to have no central concepts or set of generally used research paradigms.

The Connection with Information Systems Practice

In a rapidly changing field, there is a tendency to describe current practice rather than teaching underlying principles. There is a feeling of need to have students learn what is happening on the job rather than teaching them principles and underlying knowledge that will aid them in life-long learning. This is an ever-present danger in information systems, and may cause observers to label the field vocational rather than academic.

THE ACADEMIC ANTECEDENTS AND
BEGINNINGS OF INFORMATION SYSTEMS

Where were information system principles taught before there was an information systems field? And when computers and information systems began to emerge, which academic fields taught at least part of the material? The history of the information systems field has been detailed by Dickson (1981).

Accounting

Accounting provides a financial information system for an organization. The processing procedures (prior to computers) were termed "bookkeeping" if they were simple and "accounting systems" if they were more complex. Neither bookkeeping nor accounting systems were part of the intellectual, academic field of accounting.

A basic decision of the field of accounting as an academic discipline emerged in the early 1930s. It was to emphasize fundamental principles based on economics and to deemphasize processing procedures. Under this approach, a student in accounting could graduate without ever studying the processing procedures (the bookkeeping or systems). T-accounts were used as a useful instructional aid, but some textbooks even eliminated this connection to the processing system. In terms of the intellectual development of the field, the decision to teach accounting in a processing-free environment was a wise one. There was periodic discussion in the field that accountants should take a systems course, but the systems course was generally of poor quality and poor intellectual content. Studets found it easier to learn this material on the job. With a good conceptual grasp of the process of accounting, students found little difficulty in learning the accounting systems they found in practice. The reason for this was that the processing procedures were visible and stable.

Another limitation of accounting with respect to information systems was the historical emphasis of accounting on measurement and reporting for external reporting purposes. A recognition that external reports were inadequate for managerial purposes lead to the development of managerial accounting with emphasis on relevant costs. However, an underlying concept of both managerial and financial accounting is the rational human with unlimited information processing capabilities. Some accountants began to examine these assumptions in the areas of budgets and reports. Behavioral accounting is an accepted area of academic accounting research, but it has made little impact in main line accounting instruction. On balance, accounting had defined its domain of interest too narrowly to include the broad scope of information systems.

Management Science

Operations research, quantitative analysis, and decision sciences were another academic antecedent to information systems. Many of the methods of management science were available before computers, but they became feasible with the advent of computers. Other methods were developed because of the availability of computers. As a result, modeling, linear programming, sampling, etc., became a part of the tools taught to business students, and these tools require computers to be feasible. Students in marketing, finance, etc., are taught skills of analysis that required computers. Financial databases have become an integral part of the training for financial analysts and business planners. As users of computers, management sciences had an interest in information systems,

but much of what has come to be part of informtion systems was outside the domain of management sciences.

The Beginnings of Computer Instruction
In the Business School

The first computers were used in business organizations in the United
States in 1954 (earlier in Great Britian) for payroll processing. However,
the introduction of the IBM 1401 in 1961 followed by the IBM System/
360 in 1966 mark the real change in organizational use of computers.
The first uses were for well-defined accounting applications, but thoughtful information systems personnel were proposing more comprehensive
information systems to incorporate management science techniques
and provide better, more timely information for management.

During this time, the instruction that students received in the business
schools was oriented to the capabilities of computers and how computers
were programmed. There was much emphasis on punched card processing.
Students often learned FORTRAN. I wrote my first book, *Introduction
to Electronic Computers,* in 1966, and I had significant emphasis on
basic technology plus FORTRAN and COBOL. There were workbooks
for four major systems: IBM 1401, IBM 7094, IBM 1620, and IBM System/
360. The idea that students should learn about the computer in an organizational context rather than in a programming context started to
emerge. My next book, *Computer Data Processing,* published in 1969,
reflected a move in this direction. The field of EDP auditing was defined in a report issued by the American Institute of Certified Public
Accountants in 1968, Davis, *Auditing & EDP.*

The First Information Systems Degree Programs

The academic study of information systems began in various schools
with one or more faculty members teaching about computers and then
formulating some information systems concepts. Perhaps the first major
effort associated with a degree was the Management Information Systems
major in the Masters degree program in the School of Business at the
University of Minnesota. There were three of us who took a leadership
role in getting it going: Tom Hoffmann, Gary Dickson, and myself. The

starting date was 1968. We obtained curriculum approval and assembled a faculty group from interested faculty members. We had no special funding for anything.

The Management Information Systems Research Center (MISRC) was established at Minnesota because we felt the need for close cooperation with the information systems managers of the large companies in the Twin Cities area. We asked them for more than financial support; we asked for their participation in research and development of an educational program. The MISRC was the first of several cooperative projects of this type. We hosted the first meeting of the Society for Management Information Systems (now called the Society for Information Management). We enrolled doctoral students and began the process of developing an academic discipline.

The Decision Support System (DSS) Contender

The variety of names used for information systems instruction was described earlier. One major contender for an alternative academic program was the decision support system or DSS movement. The management information system domain was generally described to include computer-based support systems, but organizations frequently used the term to describe routine reporting and retrieval systems. A number of faculty in information systems articulated support systems for decision making and defined this as the successor to the management information system concept for an organization. They proposed that DSS be the core of information systems as an academic discipline.

The central tendency in information systems is to accept the original concept of a comprehensive information system (management information system) that includes DSS as one component. This is reflected in a recent article by McLean. Figure 1 from the article shows the relationship of EDP, DSS, and MIS as concepts in information systems.

THE DOMAIN OF INFORMATION SYSTEMS

The domain of information systems as an academic discipline is defined by the characteristics of the information system, the processes for developing and managing the information system, and the body of

FIGURE 1

Relation among EDP, MIS, and DSS from Ephraim R. McLean, "Decision Support Systems and Managerial Decision Making" in E. H. Boehm and M. K. Buckland (Eds.), *Education Information Management: Directions for the Future*, International Academy at Santa Barbara, 1983.

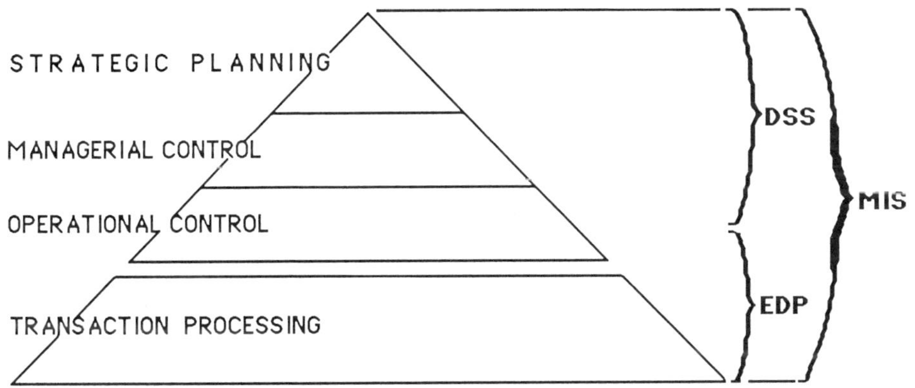

knowledge that forms the concepts foundations. Some of the domain is unique to information systems or uniquely formulated by information systems; other parts of the domain intersect with other disciplines.

Domain Based on the Characteristics of the Information System

In the late 1960s when the field began to emerge, certain concepts were central to the definition of the field. Information was viewed as an organizational resource on a par with land, labor, and capital. Information systems captured, processed, stored, retrieved, and displayed data. Data in a form useful to the recipient was recognized as being information. A frequently citied definition of an information system for an organization (or management information system) is the following:

an integrated, user machine system for providing information to support the operations, management, analysis, and decision-making functions in an organization. The system uses computer hardware and software; manual procedures; models for analysis, planning, control, and decision making; and a database. [Davis and Olson (1985) as modified from Davis (1974)].

The elements of the definition define the domain of the field as defined by the characteristics of the system which results from information systems development:

- *User-machine system.* The information system is not just computers; it combines information processing capabilities of humans and machines in preparing and using information. The information system, composed of computer technology and human participants, is a system that follows the principles defined by general systems theory. It is also an artifact that can be studied in terms of theories of living systems (Miller, 1978).

- *Supports operations, management, analysis and decision-making functions in an organization.* The context of information systems is organizations and the functions of organizations. Knowledge of the use of information in carrying out operations, in managing, and performing analysis and decision-making is required in order to design information systems.

- *Computer hardware and software.* There could be information systems without computers, but computers facilitate much more complex, interesting, and useful information systems. Information systems without computers are to computer-based information systems as oxcarts are to airplanes.

- *Manual procedures.* The design of human user procedures is vital to the success of information systems. Just as software engineering is a basis for programming, human engineering and knowledge work principles are bases for the design of user procedures for information systems.

- *Models for analysis, planning, control, and decision making.* There are a variety of models that may be used. For example, to support decision making, some may be highly structured and programmed into application systems; other unstructured decisions may be aided by decision support systems.

- *Databases.* The concept of data as an organizational resource is made operational by databases and database system technology. There may be a computer-based information system without databases and database systems, but the full concept cannot be achieved without them.

Domain Based on Information Systems Development and Management Processes

Some information systems development and management processes are unique to information systems; others are known in allied disciplines but have special formulations for the information processing field.

- *Information Systems Planning. The development* of the information system strategic plan is an instance of strategic planning, but it has unique characteristics based on the need to derive the information system plan and the information system architecture from the organizational plan. This requires an identification of organizational information needs and requirements. The plan requires consideration of future technology availability and cost. Examples of models for use in strategic planning for the information system of an organization are the Nolan stage hypothesis (best understood as a model of organizational learning) and the McFarlan and McKenney model of strategic choices (1983). Various methods of allocating resources are used to set priorities for application development or enhancement (Bowman, Davis, Wetherbe, 1981).

- *Information Requirements Determination.* Information requirements must be obtained before an information system plan may be prepared or an information system application may be developed. There are a large number of techniques and methods for information requirements determination; the selection of techniques in a specific situation is based on a contingency theory (Davis, 1982).

- *Application Development and Maintenance Process.* Based on information requirements, applications are developed or enhanced. Some of the processes that are part of application development and maintenance are:

  - *Development Methodologies.* Development procedures are used to assure that information system applications meet user requirements. The most common development methodology uses the life cycle as the basis for management, but other alternatives such as prototyping are also recommended in certain types of applications (Naumann, Davis, and McKeen, 1981).

— *Software Engineering.* The body of knowledge defines the processes to design and develop computer programs that produce complete and correct results and are maintainable. This includes the writing of computer programs.

— *Human Interface Design.* The process includes the design of screens, reports, and procedures to effectively interface with humans, so that human capabilities are enhanced and human limitations are minimized.

— *Implementation.* Implementing systems so that they will be accepted requires procedures to unfreeze existing systems, introduce new systems, and refreeze (Ives and Olson, 1982).

- *Expert Systems.* This is a subfield in cognitive psychology and artificial intelligence. Expert systems are applications that model the behavior of experts and thus provide support for non-experts in performing the same tasks.

- *Information Systems Organization and Management.* Information system organization and management has unique organizational design, controls, staffing, training, and career development issues. Information system quality assurance, backup, recovery, security, etc., are part of the information system management function.

Domain Based on Conceptual Foundations for Information Systems

The conceptual foundations for information systems are those bodies of knowledge that underlie the design and development of information systems. The conceptual foundations differ from application area knowledge. It may be important to understand accounting (application area knowledge) in order to implement accounting information system applications, but the concept of a system (fundamental conceptual foundation) underlies all applications.

- *Decision Making Processes.* Various models of decision making, methods for deciding among alternatives, and impact of individual differences on decision making are required in order to design decision support systems. This foundation includes economic behavior of the firm.

- *Concepts of Information.* What is information and what are its characteristics? There are several concepts that are useful: the mathematical theory of communication, data reduction, quality of information, and age of information.
- *Humans as Information Processors.* This area includes humans as information processors, limits on human processing, feedback, effect of data compression, and value of unused information. Much of this relates to cognitive psychology.
- *System Concepts.* Information systems are systems. They are designed using fundamental system concepts of subsystems, control, etc. The application systems, through their life, demonstrate many of the characteristics of living systems in terms of the response to stress.
- *Concepts of Planning and Control.* The organization and operation of these activities and the use of information in performing them. Human behavior affecting planning and control activities.
- *Organizational Structure and Management.* The design of organizations and organizational dynamics. These factors affect the design of information systems and the need for information in an organization.

THE TECHNOLOGY CONNECTION

In defining the domain, computer hardware and software (and related subjects) are important constituents. They represent powerful forces in bringing about the new field of information systems. Without the technology, there would not have been the new field. Even though technology represents only one part of the domain of knowledge for information system, it is a part of the core knowledge. The technology is important because it has set operational boundaries for the field. Pre-computer technology allowed only manual or bookkeeping machine information processing systems, and the boundaries of the field were very small. Not much was conceived of because not much could be implemented. Each new advance in the technology has extended the boundaries of the field because with each advance in technology, the possibilities for the information system have been expanded.

An understanding of the role of the technology in allowing a narrow, relatively uninteresting area to become one of the most exciting and intellectually challenging areas of endeavor is useful in understanding the current interest in the automated office. Office systems have been important but have not been part of the research interests of the universities. With the advent of the personal workstation, electronic mail, etc., the automated office has become a respectable area for research.

THE NECESSITY FOR INFORMATION SYSTEMS SEPARATE FROM COMPUTER SCIENCE

It is obvious that information systems and computer science are related; there is a strong area of intersection. Why shouldn't they be combined into one area—conputer science. The computer science field could have options for further study—robotics, artificial intelligence, software engineering, information systems, etc. There are good reasons why information systems should not be part of such an arrangement.

The most significant reason for the separation is that information systems is not an extension of computer science; information systems is an extension of the study of organizations, organizational systems, organizational behavior, organizational functions, and management. The nature of the extension is conditioned on the same technology that motivates computer science, but computer science is not an extension of electrical engineering (circuit design); rather it is an extension of mathematics and algorithmic processes.

Starting from such divergent beginnings, computer science and information systems have different academic cultures. Those from an algorithmic culture have a difficult time relating to organizational issues that cannot be defined with clear and complete models. The "buyer" for the product of the two fields is not the same; appropriate research is not defined in the same way; and approaches to problem solving are different.

The need for a separation of the two fields is really a need for different academic homes, but the intersection of the two fields is sufficiently large to call for significant cooperation and interactions.

THE SUBFIELDS WITHIN
INFORMATION SYSTEMS

Information systems as an academic discipline is very large and somewhat unbounded, yet reasearchers must focus on subsets of the large, ill-defined domain. Culnan used citation analysis to discover the subfields and identify the reference disciplines, Culnan (1984). Four subfields were identified as being the subject of current research: MIS management philosophy of information systems, local government systems, and implementation/DDS. The results suggested a new discipline without strong ties to reference disciplines. My observation of faculty research behavior and the selections of supporting programs and research topics by the 25 active MIS doctorial students at Minnesota suggest different results than those reported by Culnan.

There are five major subfields for academic research and expertise: information systems organization and management, design and implementation of applications, development of applications, database design and development, and specific application systems. The underlying disciplines for these are the fields of sociology, psychology, organization and management (including organizational behavior), decision science (by whatever name), computer science and artificial intelligence. Of some relevance are political science, economics, and communications. Some of these underlying body of knowledge relevant for information systems;

The following are my subfields in information systems and aligned with each are the reference disciplines that usually relate to the subfield.

Subfields in Information Systems	Reference Disciplines
Information systems organization and management	Organization and management
	Organizational sociology
Examples:	Organizational psychology
Information system planning	Organizational behavior
Information systems architecture	
Information system organization	

Design and implementation of applications   Sociology (social systems)
  Examples: Psychology (human factors)
   Decision support systems   Psychology (group behavior)
   Office systems   Psychology (expertise)
   Socio-technical design   Artificial intelligence
   Human interface design   Organizational behavior
   Expert Systems   Political science (organizational politics)
   Change management   Communications

Development of information system applications   Computer science (software engineering)
  Examples: Computer science (system software)
   Program design
   Development tools
   Quality assurance
   Maintenance

Database design and development   Computer science (database)
  Examples: Decision sciences (models)
   Data modeling
   Physical design algorithms

Application systems   Specific to application area
  Examples:
   Expert systems in specific domains
   Accounting systems
   MRP systems

SIGNS OF AN ACADEMIC DISCIPLINE

I have been a participant in much that has happened academically in information systems in the past 17 years, and I have been an observer of the rest. There is little question in my mind but that the field has moved from a loose collection of interested faculty to a fairly cohesive field with good signs of all that it takes to have an academic discipline.

There have been reasonable attempts to define curricula; scholarly journals have been established; conferences are being held regularly; "old scholar" networks have been established; and faculty members are being promoted on the basis of their scholarship in information systems.

Curriculum Recommendations

Curriculum recommendations are an important ingredient in an academic discipline because they indicate reasonable agreement as to the academic content of the field. The earliest curriculum study was the ACM report of 1972 (The Teichroew Committee report), Ashenhurst, 1972 and Couger, 1973. Two recent curriculum reports for information systems are significant:

- DPMA Model Curriculum for Undergraduate Computer Information Systems Education, edited by David R. Adams and Thomas H. Athey, 1981, Data Processing Management Association Education Foundation, 505 Busse Highway, Park Ridge, Illinois 60068.
- Information Systems Curriculum Recommendations for the 80s: Undergraduate and Graduate Programs—A Report of the ACM Curriculum Committee on Information Systems, by Jay F. Nunamaker, Jr., J. Daniel Couger, and Gordon B. Davis, 1982, Education Board of the Association for Computing Machinery, 11 West 42nd Street, New York, New York 10036.

The International Federation for Information Processing (IFIP) also produced an information systems curriculum. It is currently in the final stages of a revision.

Doctoral programs do not tend to be codified in the same way as undergraduate or Masters degree programs, but a reasonable consensus appears in various ways. The doctoral student consortium is an important quality-raising mechanism in many traditional disciplines; a doctoral student consortium is now a regular part of the Conference on Information Systems (with separate funding from the Society for Information Management).

Scholarly Journals and a Scholarly Cited Literature

There must be scholarly journals in order to have an academic discipline. The *MIS Quarterly* is the top ranked journal by information system academics; other desirable outlets for scholarly work are *Communications of the ACM, Management Science,* a number of other journals published by ACM, and some IFIP and North-Holland journals.

Publication in information systems practitioner journal of papers written by academics is to be encouraged in a field such as information systems in which innovation is frequently initiated by practitioners. In the traditional scoring system of academics, such practitioner journals count much less toward promotion. I have argued for more weight in the information systems field. The *Harvard Business Review* has frequent articles on information systems topics, and I argue a good article there has as much scholarly merit as one in *Management Science.* Not everyone agrees with me. *Datamation* has a role in the field that is somewhat unique; it has a wide range of types of articles, but the overall quality is very good. Thus, I encourage publication in it. There are also the journals such as *Data Management* and *Journal of Systems Management* that are practitioner journals associated with an information systems organization.

Hamilton and Ives (1983) have reported on the knowledge utilization among MIS researchers. They observe that "changes in critical indicators over time reveal a maturation process within the MIS literature but also highlight certain significant barriers to the efficient flow of knowledge." Of interest to me is their identification of four highly cited books and reports:

Anthony, *Planning and Control Systems: A Framework for Analysis,* Harvard University Press, Cambridge, Mass., 1965.

Blumenthal, *Management Information Systems: A Framework for Planning and Development,* Prentice-Hall, Englewood Cliffs, N.J., 1969.

Davis, *Management Information Systems: Conceptual Foundations, Structure and Development,* McGraw-Hill, New York, 1974. The second with Olson, 1985.

McKinsey, *Unlocking the Computer's Profit Potential,* New York, 1968.

These highly cited works (and 15 highly cited journal articles) also provide some insight into the field.

Conferences for Information Systems Scholars

There is no lack of conferences for computers and information systems. The National Computer Conference is comprehensive, but those wishing to emphasize information systems can be quickly lost in the crowd. The ACM National Conference is smaller, but only part of the emphasis can be on information systems. The Data Processing Management Association (DPMA) and Society for Information Management (SIM) conferences are oriented to practitioners. That leaves the Conference on Information Systems (late November or early December) and special conferences such as ISECON (Information Systems Education Conference). The net result is that information systems academics have places to meet that are relevant to the discipline.

Old Scholar Networks in Recruiting and Promotion

There have developed networks of information system professors who know each other and will respond with truthful information to calls about recruiting and promotion. This type of network also supports the development of strong scholarly activities.

Although there have been some notable failures in promotion of information system academics, a careful study of the cases suggests that the real causes are with the individual schools rather than being a sign of underlying failures, On the other hand, there is still some uncertainty among our faculty colleagues about what constitutes good information systems research and where such research is published. This was expressed a few months back when a scholar in marketing commented on a promotion case for a professor who had a reputation in data structures. He did't understand what the research was about, and the information systems faculty members either explained it so simply that it sounded trivial, or they explained it so that no one outside the field could understand it.

CENTRAL TENDENCIES IN INFORMATION
SYSTEMS RESEARCH

Some issues related to information systems research are the research paradigms for the field, the models for research, and the current research interests of the information systems academics.

Research Paradigms for the Field

Research strategies in information systems follow traditional methods. The following is a classification of 331 information systems dissertations written in the period from 1973 through 1979 (Ives, Hamilton, and Davis, 1980):

Strategy	Number	Percent
Data-based Studies:		
Case studies	46	13.9
Field studies	102	30.8
Field test	6	1.8
Laboratory study	45	13.6
Subtotal	199	60.1
Non-Data Studies	101	30.5
Unknown	31	9.4
Total	331	100.0

The research strategies and research paradigms are not new to information systems, but the variety of paradigms accepted by the field is quite large. The one approach that has been suggested that is not in widespread use in other disciplines in action research in which the researcher is a participant rather than a detached observer of the process being studied.

From an academic discipline standpoint, the percentage of non-data studies is too high. These are generall descriptive studies of current practice or descriptions of systems to be developed. Analysis of dissertations subsequent to 1979 indicates the percentage of non-data research is dropping.

There is a need to build a cumulative research tradition, and this is appearing. An example is the set of experiments termed "the Minnesota experiments" (Chervany, Dickson, and Senn, 1977). This set has caused a large number of replications and follow-on studies, so that there is a cumulative effect.

Models and Frameworks for Research in Information Systems

Several authors have conceptualized information systems research models. Examples are:

- Mason & Mitroff
- Chervany, Dickson, and Kozar
- Lucas
- Mock
- Gorry and Scott Morton
- Wetherbe and Nolan
- Ives, Hamilton, and Davis

These are summarized in Ives, Hamilton, and Davis, 1980 and Wetherbe and Nolan 1980. Two of them illustrate the nature of the research frameworks.

Mason and Mitroff (1973) view an information system as:

1. A *person* of a certain *psychological type* who
2. faces a *problem*
3. within some *organizational context* for which he needs
4. *evidence* to arrive at a solution, where the evidence is
5. made available through some *mode of presentation*

Ives, Hamilton, and Davis (1980) describe the information system research model as consisting of (Figure 2):

A. Environmental variables
   1. External environment
   2. Organizational environment

    3. User environment
    4. IS development environment
    5. IS operations environment

B. The information subsystem
    1. Content variables
    2. Presentation from variables
    3. Time of presentation variables

C. Process variables
    1. Development process
    2. Operations process
    3. Use process

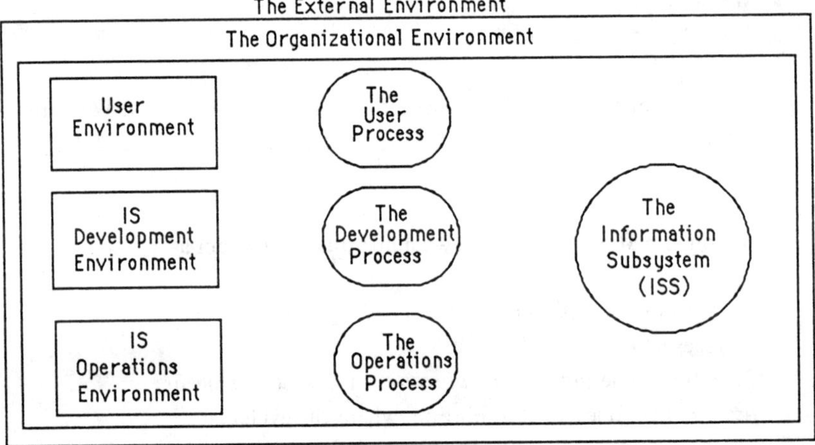

Figure 2:   A Model for Information System Research. (From Blake Ives, Schoot Hamilton, and Gordon B. Davis, "A Framework for Research in Computer-Based Management Information Systems," *Management Science,* September 1980, Vol. 25, No. 9, page 917.)

The research models and frameworks are useful in defining research, specifying variables, and in developing a research tradition.

Research Centers for Information Systems

Starting with Minnesota in 1968, a number of major information systems programs at universities have organized research centers to support information systems research. Following the Minnesota model, most of the research centers have a strong connection with the information systems practitioners. Some examples of the major research centers are:

- Management Information Systems Research Center, University of Minnesota, Graduate School of Management, Minneapolis, Minnesota.
- Center for Information Systems Research, Massachusetts Institute of Technology, Sloan School of Management, Cambridge, Massachusetts.
- Information Systems Research Associates at McMaster, McMaster University, Faculty of Business, Hamilton, Ontario Canada.
- Center for Information Studies, University of California, Los Angeles, Graduate School of Management, Los Angeles, California.
- Center for Research on Information Systems, New York University, Graduate School of Business Administration, New York, New York.
- Information Systems Research Center, University of Houston, College of Buiness Administration, Houston, Texas.
- Center for the Study of Data Processing, Washington University, St. Louis, Missouri.

Research Interests of Information Systems Faculty

In preapring the 1983 MISRC/McGraw-Hill Directory of MIS Faculty, we asked the 517 faculty to list three research interests (in their own words). An analysis of the terms they used provides some insight into the research interests of the faculty in information systems.

Term Used in a Research Interest	Number Using	Percent Using
System(s)	332	64
Information	161	31

Terms Used in a Research Interest	Number Using	Percent Using
Computer	132	26
Data (including database)	100	19
Analysis	79	15
Design	115	22
Decision support or DSS	123	24
Artificial (intelligence)	13	3
Human	31	6
Behavior	16	3
User	38	7
Control	41	8
Audit	37	7
Security	15	3
Database	78	15
Distributed	26	5
Network	21	4
Office (automation)	40	8
Micro	36	7
Graphic	18	3

SUMMARY AND FUTURE DIRECTIONS

There has been a period of less than 20 years of academic development for information systems as a discipline. Although there are close to 1000 academics who identify with information systems, less than half have been trained in information systems. Only a small number have been trained in a combination of information systems and appropriate reference discipline. However, the trend has been established, and the signs of an academic discipline have appeared: the scholarly network, conferences, journals, research centers, research frameworks, and research paradigms.

The domain of the academic discipline of information systems can be approached in several ways. The paper uses the definition of an information system, the development and management processes, and conceptual foundations to provide boundaries for the academic study of information systems.

REFERENCES

Adams, David R., and Thomas A. Athey, Editors. *DPMA Model Curriculum for Undergraduate Computer Information Systems Education.* Park Ridge, Illinois: Data Processing Management Association Education Foundation, Committee on Curriculum Development, 1981.

Ashenhurst, R., Editor. "Curriculum Recommendations for Graduate Professional Programs in Information Systems," *Communications of the ACM,* May 1971, Vol. 15, No. 5, pp. 364-398.

Bowman, B., G.B. Davis, and J. C. Wetherbe, "Modeling for MIS," *Datamation,* July 1981, pp. 155-164.

Couger, J. D., Editor. "Curriculum Recommendations for Undergraduate Programs in Information Systems," *Communications of the ACM,* December 1973, Vol. 16, No. 12, pp. 727-749.

Culnan, Mary J. "The Intellectual Structure of Management Information Systems, 1972-1982: A Co-citation Analysis," unpublished paper, School of Library and Information Studies, University of California, Berkley, California, 1984.

Davis, Gordon B. *Management Information Systems: Conceptual Foundations Structure, and Development.* New York: McGraw-Hill Book Company, 1974.

Davis, Gordon B. "Strategies for Information Requirements Determination," *IBM Systems Journal,* 1981a, Vol. 21, No. 1, pp. 4-30.

Davis, Gordon B. "The Education of Information Systems Educators," *Interface,* December 1979, Vol. 1, No. 4, pp. 8-11.

Davis, Gordon B. "The Knowledge and Skill Requirements for the Doctorate in MIS," Minneapolis: Management Information Systems Research Center Working Paper 81-12 (1981b).

Davis, Gordon B., and Margrethe H. Olsen. *Management Information Systems: Conceptual Foundations, Structure, and Development,* Second Edition. New York: McGraw-Hill Book Company, 1985.

DeGross, Janice I., Gordon B. Davis, and Gary W. Dickson. *1983 Directory of Management Information Systems Faculty.* New York: McGraw-Hill Book Company, 1983. (Available through the Management Information Systems Research Center, 93 Blegan Hall, University of Minnesota, 269 19th Avenue South, Minneapolis, Minnesota 55455. (Cost: $10.00)

Dickson, Gary W. "Management Information Systems: Evolution and Status." In M. Yovits, *Advances in Computers.* New York: Academic Press, 1981, Vol. 20, pp. 1-37.

Dickson, G., N. Chervany, and J. Senn. "Research in MIS: The Minnesota Experiments," *Management Science,* May 1977, Vol. 23, No. 9, pp. 913-923.

Hamilton, Schott, and Blake Ives. "Knowledge Utilization Among MIS Researchers," *MIS Quarterly,* December 1982, Vol. 6, No. 4, pp. 61-77.

Ives, Blake, Scott, Hamilton, and Gordon B. Davis. "A Framework for Research in Computer-Based Management Information Systems," *Management Science,* September 1980, Vol. 26, No. 9, pp. 910-934.

Ives, Blake, and Margrethe H. Olson. "User Involvement in Information Systems Development: A Review of Research," New York University Working Paper Series, December 1982.

Mason, R. O., and I. I. Mitroff. "A Program for Research on Management Information Systems," *Management Science,* 1973, Vol. 19, No. 5, pp. 475-485.

McFarlan, F. Warren, James L. McKenney, and Philip Pyburn. "The Information Archipelago—Plotting a Course," *Harvard Business Review,* January-February 1983, pp. 145-156.

McLean, Ephraim R. "Decision Support Systems and Managerial Decision Making," *Spectrum,* July/August 1984, Vol. 1. No. 2.

Miller, James Grier. *Living Systems.* New York: McGraw-Hill Book Company, 1978.

Naumann, J. David, Gordon B. Davis, and James D. McKeen. "Determining Information Requirements: A Contingency Method for Selection of a Requirements Assurance Strategy," *The Journal of Systems and Software,* 2, 1980, pp. 273-281.;

Nunamaker, Jay F., Jr. "Educational Programs in Information Systems: A Report of the ACM Curriculum Committee on Information Systems," *Communications of the ACM,* March 1981, Vol. 24, No. 3, pp. 124-133.;

Nunamaker, Jay F., Jr., J. Daniel Couger, and Gordon B. Davis. "Information System Curriculum Recommendations for the 80s: Undergraduate and Graduate Programs—A Report of the ACM Curriculum Committee on Information Systems," *Communications of the ACM*, November 1982, Vol. 25, No. 11, pp. 781-805.

Wetherbe, James C., and Gordon B. Davis. "Developing a Long-Range Information Architecture," *Proceedings of the National Computer Conference*, Anaheim, California, May 1983, AFIPS Press, Vol. 52.

Wetherbe, James C., and Richard L. Nolan. "Toward a Comprehensive Framework for MIS Research, *MIS Quarterly*, June 1980, Vol. 4, No. 2.

Michael Buckland

EMERGING COMMONALITIES:
LIBRARY SYSTEMS, RECORD MANAGEMENT,
AND MANAGEMENT INFORMATION SYSTEMS

INTRODUCTION

My assignment is to examine whether there are emerging commonalities among the three fields of library systems, records management, and management information systems and what these commonalities might be. In doing this, three approaches will be used: the perspective of the Information Institute Conference on Education for Information Management at Santa Barbara (1983); a theoretical view of these fields in relation to information studies generally; and a pragmatic view of how some commonalities appear to be emerging in practice.

THE SANTA BARBARA CONFERENCE

It would be an exaggeration to state that there was a unified perspective at this conference. However, the perspective that was underlying the planning of the conference did have some identified elements (Buckland 1983a):

i) That the quantities of recorded information available will continue to increase substantially.

ii) That information—recorded information—has and will continue to become more significant as planning, engineering, administration, and other activities that shape our lives become wider in scope, deeper in complexity, less grounded in common experience, and more dependent upon information.

iii) There has been and there will continue to be a proliferation and diversification of information-related occupational roles.

iv) There has been and there will continue to be a shift from the technology of paper to the technology of computer—moving toward increasingly versatile workstations.

v) Paradoxically, there appears to be also a degree of convergence among information professionals as each becomes more sophisticated in what he or she does:

a) At a conceptual level the creation, storage, organization, and retrieval of records is common to several activities even though the individuals performing those activities have tended to view these as quite different: library services, museum documentation, database directory design, records management, etc.

b) At a technical level the same sorts of electronic hardware and even software are being used for different activities.

c) At an organizational level there are some indications of a trend to bring together at least some information support activities under the direction of someone with the title of Vice President for Information Management or similar.

vi) It was also asserted that, in a changing world, teaching even the best contemporary practice is not good enough if one is seeking to develop professionals who will design new services and adapt old ones as needs, circumstances, and opportunities change. One needs to deal with concepts and principles as well as practice; *and* one needs to foster respect for the uniqueness of each situation.

The conference was, in fact, remarkable for the diversity of constituencies represented and the papers and the discussions offered a kaleidoscope of views. They did not,however, refute the six assumptions underlying the planning, but rather, illustrated the rich complexity of our concerns and the potential for dialog that our parochial pursuits have tended to lack.

STUDIES OF INFORMATION

As a second perspective on the commonalities of these three fields we might try to delineate in general terms the region that they occupy within the broader reaches of information studies and to examine the characteristics of the region.

Information studies, broadly interpreted, are very extensive in scope: A wide variety of activities and disciplines are concerned with information in one way or another: linguistics, cognitive science, cybernetics, artificial intelligence . . . and so on.

I have found it helpful to think in terms of two levels of information studies. In the broader sense of information studies we are concerned with representations of knowledge, both representations in the abstract sense ("text," whether prose, numbers, or image) and physical manifetations of these representations ("text-bearing objects"). (Wilson, 1968).

Within the broad and amorphous realm of information studies, we can usefully distinguish a more specific area of concern: the identification, description, manipulation, storage, retrieval, and use of representations of knowledge—of information.

The processes of arrangement, description, and retrieval, in particular, imply the creation and use of *representations* of knowledge. The card catalog in a library is a familiar example of the representation of representations of knowledge. A central, unifying concern, then, for our three specialities is with information retrieval. This includes the principles of indexing, classification, content analysis and description, and similar sorts of activity, including both techniques for storage and strategies for retrieval. This is certainly true of library systems, records management, and management of information systems.

Yet information retrieval, although central and unifying, is not our only concern. In order to see information retrieval properly in context we also need to interest ourselves with information studies in the broader sense of concern with representations of knowledge, with knowledge itself, and, indeed, with people insofar as their needs are related through knowledge and representations of knowledge to information retrieval.

The actual and potential contexts for study defined in this way are very extensive, including documentation in numerous specialized areas:

museums, engineering, litigation, bureaucracies, . . . Nor is the field restricted to document retrieval systems: data retrieval and "knowledge availability systems" are also included. Meanwhile, technological changes, notably computers and telecommunications, continue to cause profound change because of the flexibility, manipulative power, decentralization, and opportunities for observation that they permit.

As an initial simplification, it is helpful to view this field as containing three quite different and loosely connected sorts of processes (Buckland, 1983b):

1. *Cognitive and epistemological processes*

Inquiry: What are the origins, causes, and motivations behind the inquiries that arise which information systems could be expected to help with? How can future inquiries be predicted? What determines when an inquiry is satisfied or abandoned?

Becoming informed: How does the output yielded by information systems affect the knowledge of the individuals using the system? How can the presentation of the output be related to the knowledge of the inquirer?

The study of information leads rapidly to severe difficulties *because* it has to do with human knowledge. For example, scientists used to "know" that the earth was the center of the universe and were so informed by books in libraries. We are dealing, therefore, with beliefs rather than some concrete disembodied knowledge.

2. *Retrieval processes*

Design of the information system includes systems for the selection, organization, and retrieval of the information to be stored and of the attributes that are to be used as a basis for retrieval—and the retrieval rules by which the system would work.

The transformation of inquiries into formal searches means "translating" the inquiry into the "language" of the system—an acute human-system interface problem.

Response and responsiveness. How well does the system yield what it is supposed to retrieve? By what criteria should the information system by judged? Inconsistent use of the the term "relevance" illustrates well some of the problems here, notably the difference between the technical *capability* (responsiveness) of an information system and the *utility* (in human values) of its use. The difference is highly significant (Buckland, 1983c).

3. *The provision and use of information systems.*

Demand: Although impulses to use information derive from a desire to know something, the actual expressed demand is a product of a wide variety of factors. Use appears to depend on the individual's perception of the probably real price (time, effort, discomfort, money) of using an information system, compared with alternative means of solving, evading, or ignoring the problem.

The *provision* of information systems depends heavily on perceptions of their appropriateness and usefulness, not only in the eyes of the users but also in the view of those who provide the resources, who are commonly different people: What good does it do? Whose values determine what constitutes beneficial effects? How are these values derived and changed?

In addition to the study of these sorts of processes, there is a need to study the *structure* of the parts within and between the processes. In what sorts of ways do they form systems? What are the dynamics of the interactions?

In discussing this conceptual perspective I have made no explicit reference to library systems, records management, or information systems. Instead my purpose was to delineate in general terms the nature of the field in which I would include all three. Further analysis should then permit the implied commonalities to emerge more explicitly.

A PRAGMATIC VIEW

It may also be helpful to look more pragmatically at the three fields, to observe what has been happening in them, to speculate on how they are developing, and to postulate similarities and commonalities. Two examples will be given:

i) *The organization's systems of records*

Classical records management was concerned with the creation of records series, with rentention schedules, with vital records, with microforms, and with the disposition of records.

More recently the "life cycle" concept, the move to machine-readable records and indexes to records, and increased concern with legal aspects of privacy and of freedom of information have broadened the concerns of the records manager.

In a well-developed situation, the corporate records manager will need to be concerned with a range of records, a diversity of formats (paper, microform, machine-readable), decentralized access, and the convenience, cost, and cost-effectiveness of the organization's records. A telephone company, for example, needs to keep track of personnel, equipment, land, customers, and accounts— in great detail and on a large scale. This goes beyond what I have referred to as "classical records management" but is a natural development of it.

It seems useful to me to describe modern records management as being concerned with the *organization's system of records.*

- *"Records"* are the objects that are handled: paper, microform, machine-readable records;

- *"System"* implies complexity and relatedness. A simple transaction, such as installing or using a phone, may involve staff, a customer, an account, and equipment—and affect the records pertaining to each. The records will need to be more or less interrelated;

- *"Organization's"* implies that the system of records is purposive, that it should be useful, usable, and economical. It implies that the records management function supports and advances the technical, economic, political, and legal goals of the organization.

If this view of modern records management is correct, then it it is not difficult to imagine how it will look as modern technology comes to be applied. We have a preview of it in a rather exotic form in the example of the technical services systems that have been developed (mostly behind the scenes) in libraries. The "technical services" support system constitutes an interrelated web of complex financial, bibliographical, and other records on paper, card, printout, microform, disk, tape, memory, and screen. It includes accounting, purchasing, inventory, index (catalog), and locational (circulation) records and constitutes a significant portion of the "organization's system of records" in the case of a library. (Pemberton has also stressed the functional similarity of librarianship and records management.)

ii) *Operational, tactical and strategic information systems*

At the Santa Barbara Conference, Professor McLean described the development of Management Information Systems (MIS) and of Decision Support Systems (DSS) (McLean, 1983). A significant aspect of this development is that automated systems have lent themselves most easily not to the support of strategic decision-making but, quite the reverse, to dealing with tactical, operational, and best, transaction processing. It is not hard to see why. Computers deal best with records that are highly structured: numerical, unambigious, and fixed-field. These are the attributes of transactions and of operations, but not of strategic issues.

The president of a University, for example, should have a management information system giving details of classroom utilization, student credit-hours, faculty-student contact hours, and the like. These statistics have their place, but I would hope that the President would give greater attention to trends in society, changes in education, the local economy, and the political climate. The sources for these matters differ substantially from those of the management information system (Culnan):

- These are generally derived from *outside* the organization rather than from *within;*
- they are far typically *textual* rather than *numerical;*
- they are far *less structured-* conversations, reports, newspaper articles, fragmentary, incomplete, inconsistent statistics;
- they come in various *inconvenient forms;*
- for any given problem their *relevance and significant may be difficult to assess;*
- they tend to be *wide-ranging* in scope and *low in accuracy, currency, and frequency of use;*
- they do not lend themselves to "computing."

Support for strategic decision-making includes extensive reliance on "messy" data from the outside world and can be expected to do so increasingly in the "post-industrial" organizations (Huber). How to organize, assess, select, and retrieve messy data has always been a central problem in librarianship.

CONCLUSION

It is difficult to avoid the conclusion that commonalities are emerging among library systems, records management, and information systems. It is not, perhaps, that commonalities are emerging; but rather, as each field develops, the commonalities are coming to be recognized. Recognizing them has been hindered by the different origins, perspectives, and traditions of the three fields. All three have problems. All three are changing. Each could use any help it can derive from the others.

NOTE

The comments of Professors Mary Culnan and Partick Wilson, School of Library and Infomration Studies, University of California, Berkeley, are gratefully acknowledged.

REFERENCES

Buckland, Michael K. (1983a) "Keynote Address" In: Education for Information Management. Santa Barbara: International Academy, 1983, 13-18. See also Buckland, Michael K. "Records Management in its Intellectual Context: Experience at Berkeley." *Records Management Quarterly* 16(4) Oct 1982, 26-28, 30.

Buckland, Michael K. (1983b) *Library Services in Theory and Context.* New York: Pergamon, 1983.

Buckland, Michael K. (1983c) "Relatedness, Relevance, and Responsiveness in Retrieval Systems." *Information Processing and Management* 19(3), 1983, 237-241.

Culnan, Mary C. "Information science and the automated office: Challenges and opportunities" In: American Society for Information Science. *Proceedings of the 44th Annual Meeting, 1981.* White Plains, New York: Knowledge Industry Publications Inc., 1981, 139-141.

Education for Information Management. Conference, Santa Barbara, 1982. Edited by E. Boehm and M. K. Buckland. Santa Barbara: International Academy. 1983.

Huber, George P. "The nature and design of post-industrial organizations," *Management Science* 30(8), August 1984, 928-951.

Machlup, Fritz and Mansfield, Una, eds. *The Study of Information: Interdisciplinary Voices.* New York: Wiley, 1983.

McLean, Ephraim R. "Decision Support Systems and Managerial Decision Making." In: *Education for Information Management.* Santa Barbara: International Academy, 1983, 63-72.

Pemberton, J. Michael. "Records management courses in accredited library schools: A rationale and survey." *Records Management Quarterly* 16(3) July 1982, 10-12, 14-16.

Wilson, Patrick G. *Two Kinds of Power: An Essay on Bibliographic Control.* Berkeley: University of California Press, 1968. Chapter 1: "The Bibliographical Universe."

Joseph C. Donohue

A DISCIPLINE FOR THE
INFORMATION PROFESSIONS

We've come here to explore what information professionals need to know. Out hosts have directed our attention to three kinds of information professionals: librarians, information systems people, and information resource managers.

There are two groups of information occupations not of immediate concern to us here. One is the *creators* of the records, such as writers, publishers, and artists who record their work. The other is the *users* of the record: e.g., teachers, researchers, and practitioners of many professions.

The three occupations of special concern here, librarianship (in the broad meanings, including some other information services), information systems, and information resource management, are a good place to start our discussion, because their common involvement with management of the record is far more important than are their differences.

Their function as managers of the record isn't a trivial one, though some people think it is. For example, an art professor I knew once said that "Librarians are the camp followers of the intellectual life." He, by the way, was the curator of a gallery.

Even in the face of that kind of snobbery, many people with excellent talents and abilities have devoted themselves to the management of the human records. At this meeting we're exploring those abilities and their intellectual basis.

153

Many of us here have a primary association with one or another of the three occupations around which the conference is organized. We have a good sense of what our own kind of people do, and of our goals and values. We might assume that people from related information professions see us and our roles as we do, but that could be a mistake. We could talk and work at cross purposes unless we begin with some common view of our respective roles, or at least know where our views on that subject differ.

I'm going to begin by offering here my own view of each of the three groups, not because I think it complete and accurate, but because I'd like it to be. I see this meeting as a chance to clarify my ideas on how the three groups fit together, and in order to do so, I have to chance exposing my ignorance. I don't think my own views are necessarily typical of any of the three professional groups, because over the past thirty-some years I've worked about equally in all three. While that kind of background provides a personal perspective, it doesn't inculcate typical or orthodox attitudes.

I imagine many people here have given much thought to analyzing the functions and contributions of the three occupations we are studying. I have chosen not to begin with that kind of analysis, but rather by sharing some ideas about how the origins of those professions have affected their basic assumptions, their general approach to information management, to tools they use and how they judge results.

I will ask you to reflect that we can look at these occupations from a number of contexts, and from several points of view; and that we can avoid confusion by reminding ourselves from time to time which context and viewpoint is operating.

I will advocate that we give special attention to the *disciplinary* aspect of the three professions, as the one that can help us the most to communicate. After briefly reviewing the development of the information science discipline as I understand it, I'll offer some suggestions about how we may identify in the information professions the components of a discipline adequate to serve as their intellectual base.

LIBRARIANSHIP

In the United States, librarianship and library science in something like their present form began about a century ago. At that time, one of the biggest economic and social problems was how to absorb huge numbers of new city dwellers: people from our own country areas as well as waves of people escaping from poverty and oppression abroad. They were a motley group, in that respect, a bit like information professionals. They needed means for developing a common culture. Like schools, libraries, played an important part in their acculturation.

Some historians now argue whether the librarians were high-minded social reformers, bent on uplifting the masses, or tools of the robber barons, the mill-owners, for example, who wanted people to be able to read and write so they would be more efficient workers and would use their spare time constructively in ways such as reading books instead of drinking beer and fomenting rebellion.

Whatever their motivations, librarians helped the process of acculturation. In doing so, they also created also an aspiring *profession*, librarianship, and an aspiring *discipline*, library science.

Libraries provided employment and a self-image for many people, particularly women, whose education was general and humanistic, rather than scientific or technical, and who either because of choice or exclusion, did not enter the established professions or commerce.

The characteristics of American librarians haven't changed greatly. They still come, overwhelmingly, from the humanities, social sciences, and fields other than the natural sciences. As real people, they have their share of inadequacies, but I think they still demonstrate much concern for social service and for the human condition. Without heroics they put their values on the line day after day to the extent that they serve people's information needs, often with little recognition.

The image of the librarian is probably much of what it was a century ago: genteel, reasonably well educated, but poor and powerless. The image may be changing, but not very fast.

When a librarian's job pays well and has prestige, it still often goes to someone whose credentials have little to do with managing a library, but which carry more weight. The Librarian of Congress is not a librarian, but an historian. The Director of the National Library of Medicine has been traditionally a physician. Their credentials are not related to the practice of librarianship, though they are clearly relevant to the purpose of the libraries they direct.

But many libraries and analogous information facilities in government, industry and elsewhere report to directors with neither subject knowledge nor knowledge of libraries. By my own observation, many of them never acquire any knowledge of, or even interest in, the substantive and professional problems of library or information service. In fact, some I've worked with expressed open contempt for such concerns. Perhaps more important is that many do not share certain attitudes that the library profession at its best fosters, such as a commitment to the widest appropriate access to information, and a sensitivity to the needs of information users.

One reason why librarians do not have a better public image is that the work they do is work anyone can do badly. Sometimes when people learn that I have a degree in library science, they ask, "You gotta go to school for that?"

A related reason is that libraries are complex enough, and well enough designed, that they can be useful, even to the uninitiated, and even when they aren't running well. That isn't so with computers or TV sets, so programmers and electronics technicians have more prestige. In the absence of an expert, you can fumble around in a library and maybe find what you want. Fumble around the computer or the TV set, and you get electrocuted, or at least wipe out the picture on the tube, or worse, the memory, as I have done several times in preparing this text. Ah. That reminds me. I have to SAVE.

INFORMATION SYSTEMS
SPECIALISTS

In contrast to librarianship, information systems as a profession emerged in the 1950s and 1960s, a time marked by official concern more for military and technical problems than for social problems. World War II have accelerated the development of powerful tools, especially the computer: systems scientists, rightly, I think, point out that their discipline is not the same as computer science; yet there is an important symbiotic relation between them. It took dramatic advances in systems science to develop the computer, which thereafter became system science's most powerful tool.

The achivments of systems sciences, beginning with ballistics during wartime, proceeding to solution of complex mathematical problems in peacetime, and then revolutionizing business practices, earned for systems science and engineering an awesome respect, perhaps best illustrated by the public attention given to the moon program. The systems approach pervades much of our thought even in areas in which, to all but the true believer, it is of dubious applicability.

Efficiency, even more than effective relation to the overall environment of the system, seems to be the cherished value of systems engineering, and reverence for efficiency spills over into the rest of our society.

Perhaps we cherish efficiency all the more in recent years because the systems that affect our lives seem to be breaking down. The phrase "nothing works and nobody cares" really isn't true, though. We all want efficient systems; at least we want our systems, those that pay us off, to work. The that extent, we all respect the central value of systems science, efficiency.

Our uneasiness with the systems ethos is not, I think, with the notion of efficiency, or usually with systems engineering's ability to achieve it, but rather with the too ready adoption of goals set by other people. That's the kind of situation that promoted the phrase, coined during the heyday of both punched cards and revolt on campus: I am a human being. Do not fold, spindle, or mutilate.

INFORMATION RESOURCE
MANAGERS

Information resource management, in turn, emerged under that name in the late 1970s. *Information* management is the esential work of librarians, records managers, information systems people, and others. Information *resource* management has also occupied their attention for decades, as you can see if you read what some of them have written during that time.

But most of the people in those occupations, even when doing and thinking information resource management, haven't called it that. Many do not think of themselves primarily as managers, nor do they present themselves to the employment market as such. Some are so fascinated by the intellectual and technical challenges of their work that they pointedly prefer *not* to be managers.

We must respect their choice, but it often results in conditions they find intolerable, wherein the managers to whom they report have little or no knowledge of the problems they face, nor respect for the values they themselves hold. It seems that one has to put up or shut up—either be willing to be a manager, think like one, and act like one or else be managed by someone who does.

The self-styled information resource managers, on the other hand, see themselves primarily *as* managers, not just of information but of *resources*—facilities, people, money, equipment, systems and so on. Going a giant step further, they concern themselves explicitly with the whole *cycle of events* that results in information management, from the initial concept, to the planning and creation of an organization to provide information, to its operation, its evaluation and its adaptation to changes in its environment.

Most importantly, perhaps, they see themselves as makers of *policy* regarding the management of these resources. They intended to be in charge, and they are convincing many decision makers who appoint managers and allocate resources that they ought to be.

It is worthwhile looking carefully at the rise of the concept and of the profession of information resource manager, because it is conceptually the most inclusive of the three occupations we are discussing.

THE MANAGERIAL ETHOS

Support for the idea of comprehensive information resource management (IRM) comes in part from "scientific management," which has grown into a powerful mythology since its inception with Frederick Taylor and the Gilbreths. Scientific management did much to create acceptance for the idea of the general manager.

At an earlier time, high level managers were chosen primarily for their expertise in what may be called, for lack of a better word, "substantive" knowledge: engineering, law, finance, and the like. (The professional manager may object, with some justice, to using the word that way, because in another sense, management *is* substantive, its substance *being* management. It operates at what has sometimes been called a "meta" level, just as do librarianship and systems engineering.)

More recent is a trend towards the selection of managers whose professional training is in management *per se.* Even many general managers who have also a formal training in a substantive discipline orient themselves to management rather than to their subject discipline or profession.

From the mentality of scientific management, certain assumptions carry over into the world of information systems and services organizations, namely: that the substance or function of what is managed is trivial, in the technical sense, compared to the function of *management;* that a manager can manage anything with equal facility; and that the credentials for positions of power ought to be training and experience in management rather than in any academic, scientific, or other specialty.

MANAGERIAL VALUES

It seems likely that the viewpoint and values, as well as the conceptual tools of the manager, will differ from those of the librarian and the systems scientist. My own experience bears that out, but I find it hard to state the differences clearly, or to generalize about managers I've known.

Most "managers *per se*," whom I know, come from a background of business administration, either by virtue of formal study or of experience, or both. What are their values? Can they be characterized as a group? I don't know what systematic studies show. In thinking about the values of business, two things come to my mind, one of them historical, the other current, though it too has a history.

The historic idea is the puritan ethic, which, we've been told, was strong in the evolution of the capitalist system. I had a strong commitment to busines and wealth as *stewardship;* the manager's role was considered a "calling" and his performance was to be judged by how faithfully he discharged his responsibility to others. I may seem naive, but I believe there are still some faint vestiges of that attitude in the business ethic, usually expressed in a secular, rather than traditionally religious form.

The second idea also has history, but is currently being revived by some business theorists: that *the* purpose of business is to maximize profit, and that any diluting of that purpose is a disservice to the investor and ultimately to society. This position, I believe, is advanced on the grounds not only of expediency, but also of ethics.

What comes to mind is this: if the right value of business is to maximize wealth, is the right value of management to maximize power? Many managers I have known seem to act on that principle. And they were not all trained in schools of management. One high level librarian-manager I know, in dismissing the claims of participative management, said, "You make it all to difficult. Management is really very simple: it is imposing your will on other people."

On the other hand, I know some people whose primary orientation is to manage *per se,* whose style encourages the widespread sharing of power. I've found those sharers of power less often in government than in businesses that were highly competitive, though that may seem strange. For what it's worth, I find very few power sharers in charge of libraries, either among librarian-managers or general managers. These observations are only personal; they may not indicate any general truth. Nevertheless, I have wondered if there is something that attracts the autocrat to library management, or brings out the quality once a manager is installed.

IRM AS A RESULT OF
THE TECHNOLOGY

Another factor in the rise of IRM is the nature of the new information technology, which is both *ex*plosive in its power and *im*plosive in its effect. It is *ex*plosive in its power to change the conditions of our lives and work; *im*plosive in the ways it brings together quickly and powerfully, kinds of work that were once quite separate. Tasks once done by people with different backgrounds, training, and ranking in the organization are now combined into fewer, more complex operations.

This process reverses what mass production did to the nature of work. The factory system broke down complex operations into simpler tasks; the new information technology does the opposite. An example: in integrated office systems, the secretary's job is enhanced; she or he can now do more complex tasks than before. The manager or researcher in such a setting can also do more and be more efficient than before, though possibly at the cost of performing some tasks, such as punching a keyboard, that could previously have been delegated to others. Even that penalty will probably be removed by still later technology.

The result of implosiveness is to combine not only tasks, but also broader functions. I am told that the Apple Computer company has no secretaries, at least none by that name. For Apple, throwing out the *word* "secretary" may accompany recognition of the real importance of the essential secretarial *function,* hidden in the word "secretary": the keeper of the secrets. Some people always understood that importance, but most people made secretaries into personal servants.

Just as tasks are combined, then functions, so are departments. For example, editing and publishing functions, once part of a research department, are now often combined with computer services, the library, records management, and so on, into an "information resources" department, sometimes under that name. Some organizations go as far as to include in the same structure with these services the corporate planning and operational research functions. They too are information functions, though they relate more obviously to policy than to service.

The management of such diverse and complex activities clearly requires a high level of skill and judgement. Less certain is what special qualities of knowledge, experience, skill and temperament are most needed. Even if we assume that the trend toward the choice of the "general manager" holds true in the field of information resources, there remain questions.

Within schools of management there are specialized programs, in management information systems (MIS). Should such programs be expanded to include management of more diverse information resources, such as libraries, as well as information centers and other specialized facilities serving industry, science, consumers, and the community? Would such a trend drive the wedge deeper between managers *per se* and those with what I have called "substantive" or other professional orientation? How feasible would that be? How acceptable would it be to the people in the respective tracks?

Paperwork Reduction"

Still another factor in the rise of information resource management is the complex of conditions involving the passage of the Paperwork Reduction Act of 1980. That law would more accurately have been called the "Information Resource Management Act," because whatever reduction in paperwork it causes will be less important than its likely effect on the organization of information resources in government, and by example, in the private sector.

Paperwork reduction, to be sure, is an appropriate function of management, but certainly not the most important part. And it is not what the Act is all about. "Paperwork reduction" in the title was a political advantage: who could be against it? On the other hand, any title that spoke

of resource management, could have spooked a public that had recently
seen some pretty fancy management of information by government, in
Watergate.

I believe that there have been significant changes in the distribution
of resources and power within agencies as a result of the Act, and that it
offers the likelihood of much more. The Act mandates stronger managerial
control over all information resources.

The Act has brought to public and official attention the new role of
IRM as an important managerial function, and I think government at
state and local level will follow the federal trend. Business is already
moving that way; in fact it led the federal government, if I am not mis-
taken.

Has the Act really reduced paperwork? If so, how lasting will the result be? I cannot say. I do know that agencies have made glowing reports
about the number of cubic feet of records destroyed each year and the
filing cabinets retired. The newspaper, in interviews with federal officials
responsible for the implementation of the Act in regulatory agencies
have reported reductions in the number of forms that small business
has to fill out. In general, I think we are justified in withholding belief
for awhile. Those results may be, if you will excuse the expression, only
on paper. *The New Yorker,* to my delight, picked up on the fact that
attendees at training sessions on paperwork reduction received 1000-
page training manuals.

Three Professions; Three Contexts; Three Points of View

In examining the three information occupations, I think it useful to
remind ourselves that they operate in three *contexts:* the professional,
the disciplinary and the educational.

By the *professional,* I mean the way the occupation is organized in
the work place and in professional societies.

The *disciplinary* refers really to two different things. One is the discipline as it is parcelled out in settings such as the university. The other is
the discipline in the sense of a body of ideas that is constantly being
integrated into a coherent pattern by people interacting thoughtfully
in trying to make sense of it all. The discipline in the latter sense is not
bounded by academic organizational lines. I think we should concern

ourselves primarily with the discipline in this, to me, more meaningful sense.

Finally the *educational* context relates to schools, apprenticeships or other means the profession uses to codify the discipline and to pass it on.

There are also at least three *viewpoints* that people commonly take in discussing occupations: turf, abstraction, and function.

Turf, of course, is the question of who gets to do what, and who gets the money. We see it operating in the fights that labor organizers have about who represents the workers and collects their dues, or in the fights among deans about who gets to teach the courses that are not securely nailed down.

Though *abstraction* sounds more intellectual than turf, its quarrels are often as heated. You can observe it in disputes among scientists and scholars about the claims and limits of a particular discipline, or about which includes the other. "Is social science really science?" "Are computer science and system science the same thing?" Sometimes, of course, these debates are merely smoke screens for turf disputes, and never very good ones.

The third point of view is *functionality.* It would examine an occupation in the light of the function it performs socially, and of its results. This viewpoint would then look to what kind of knowledge is actually operating to good effect in performing the function, and where such knowledge can be obtained. I favor this viewpoint, thinking it close to common sense, though I recognize some limitations to the usefulness of even common sense. As a friend of mine often says, "That's all well and good in practice, but does it work out in theory?"

Unity or Diversity

Will information management be one profession? Will its many specialties contribute to, and draw from, a single, common discipline? Can a single type of professional school serve all those specialties, the way a medical school serves the needs of a very diverse profession?

I do not expect to see those things happen neatly. Implosion will continue in the workplace, reducing the distances among occupations, in practical ways. Positions descriptions will be combined more and more. Economic forces will result in some mergers among professional organizations, as among schools, especially the library schools, which after years

of expansion, now must either expand their mandates or close their
doors. Some are doing both, in quick succession.

What about the discipline? I do not expect to see a clearly articulated
comprehensive information discipline arise. Disciplines in the organized
academic sense are slow to change. In the second sense, that of living
tissue of ideas, they can change rapidly, and today's powerful information
technology encourages rapid change. Ease of communication is heighten-
ing the importance of the informal channels, the "invisible colleges," that
cross the borders of formal disciplines as well as of nations.

That kind of exchange has been occurring for several decades with
respect to the study of information, as some scientists, engineers, librarians, linguists, logicians, mathematicians and others interact, often explicitly under the rubric of "information science."

The Idea of an Information Science

The term of the idea of an information science is found in classical
philosophies of East and West, in their analyses of logic and their concern for a theory of knowledge. Much of the histories of both philosophy
and psychology can be seen as laying the groundwork for such a science.
Information science in today's sense, though, was born of a more practical consideration, namely the application of new technology to deal with
what has been called the "information explosion."

Nevertheless, the group organized expressly for that purpose, the
American Documentation Institute (ADI), soon broadened its concern
to include many other aspects of information, both practical and theoretical. The change was, of course, reflected in its present name, the American
Society for Information Science (ASIS).

I have found fascinating the way that shift occurred. The early concentration of ADI was mircofilm for documentary uses, lead to the common use, in this country, of "documentation" to mean the application
of newer technology to documentary problems. However, interest soon
shifted to more diverse techniques and tools for improving access to information. These techniques were dubbed "information retrieval," a term
that caught on, replacing "documentation" as the catch-phrase for the
new information technology.

I think, incidentally, that one reason the term became popular is that
it has a subtle humor about it. In fact, back in the 1960s, Don Lent, an

irreverant artist friend of mine, upon hearing the phrase, and having a distaste for jargon, designed a monument ". . . honoring the heroism of the IRA"—The Information Retrieval Agency, he explained—showing atop a pedestal, a large, scholarly-looking dog, wearing glasses, and bearing in its mouth the newspaper. Since it is also pointing with its forepay, I guess it is both a retriever *and* a pointer.

"Science Information" and "Information Science"

The newer techniques for retrieval, not surprisingly, were invented and used first in scientific and technical establishments, where there was also a lively interest in the overall problems of scientific information, including the training of science information specialists. At a conference on that latter subject, in 1964, Robert Taylor and Robert M. Hayes did much to clarify the difference between the narrower concern for serving the information problems of the sciences (science information) and the broader interests of a science *of,* or *about* information, which they identified as "information science." (Georgia 1964). Each of those men in turn served as President of the ASIS, and both did much to define what information science was and was to become.

A few years later, Harold Borko, another early President of the Society, published in its journal, a definition of the emerging discipline, as ". . . an interdisciplinary science that investigates the properties and behavior of information, and the techniques, both manual and mechanical, of processing information for optimal storage, retrieval, and dissemination."

The new discipline, Borko said, ". . . is derived from and related to such fields as mathematics, logic, linguistics, psychology, computer technology, operations research, graphic arts, communication, library science, management and other fields." (Borko 1968). The definition has been much quoted and has stood up under scrutiny in a field of interest in which few things are agreed upon. If we consider the discipline to have begun when it was thus defined and named, it is just about twenty years old.

The Record Thus Far

In its brief lifespan, information science has not established itself as a coherent or rigorous discipline. Some of its critics complain that it has produced little research, and no substantial body of theory. In an admirable review of information science research, Martha West says that the talent and energy once devoted to research shifted to applications in libraries and in the commercial sector, even while funding for research was available. (West 1983).

Hans Wellisch, after careful examination of the literature up to 1976, showed that no consensus existed about what information science (IS) is or should do; neither was there a generally accepted definition of information, its central focus. Wellisch at least allowed that the field of study, which he preferred to call "informatics," following the European usage, might possibly develop into a true science. (Wellisch 1976).

Curtis Wright, however, writing in the ASIS journal, attacked the very idea that a science of information was even theoretically possible. Information, he said, unlike the physical sciences, lies outside the range of empirical inquiry.

Though recognizing the need for understanding of both the informational functions of all human expression, and for the historical study of society's information systems, Wright contended that such understanding as may be attained must be found through philosophical, rather than scientific modes of investigation. (Wright 1979).

There is a delightful irony in a discipline's journal announcing that the discipline does not and *cannot* exist. Wright's argument is carefully constructed, but is based on some *a priori* reasoning and on a very restrictive notion of science, which information scientists do not seem to accept. I am not sure the argument was ever given the rebuttal it deserved. Most people who embrase the discipline seem to feel that if information science does not exist, it ought to be created, and, by implication, that it is possible to do so. In any case, Wright's attack seems to have made little difference.

It should surprise no one that IS is not a fully developed, rigorous science. Twenty years in the history of a discipline is a very short time. After all, physicists who could not define to their own satisfaction what electricity is, continued studying certain very mysterious phenomena, and their accomplishments are impressive.

It is too early to give up on information science, or even to judge its progress fairly, since little has been done to assess systematically the work done under its own auspices, much less the relevant contributions from its precedent and related disciplines: library science, documentation, psychology, and other fields, some of whose workers might be surprised to learn that have been doing information science.

The Value of an Even Inexact Science

Even if we do not think that a rigorous science of information is possible or likely, there is still interest and even practical value in organizing our ideas and data concerning the central theme of information into a single frame of reference, with as much exactness as possible.

There are many kinds of players in the information game. Even among the three kinds examined in this conference, not much has been done to coordinate ideas or activities. The players probably reinvent things under different names beyond the point where healthy competition spurs achievement.

Up to a point, competition has positive value; beyond that point, it can degenerate into tedious duplication of effort and petty one-upmanship. Participation in a common discipline of information, on the other hand, might lead to the kind of insights and opportunities that often lie at the boundaries of professions and disciplines.

This conference could do much to generate such insights and opportunities.

The Need for, (and Dangers of), Defining

As Wellisch pointed out, there is a danger of wasting much effort if we do not know what we are looking for. On the other hand, there is also a danger of getting bogged down right at the beginning, in irresolvable arguments about definitions. Perhaps we can find a middle ground, defining to the extent we can and need to, and making clear wherein we disagree.

Though it may not be necessary or possible to agree on what information is, in the abstract, it would help to decide which functions of the three occupations we consider essential to the information role.

We need then to define the kinds of knowledge and skills needed to perform those functions well. This seems to be the approach of King Research, in studying the educational needs of librarians. In doing so, of course, we must look truly at functions, not merely tasks. Tasks may change rapidly; functions seem more durable.

Having identified the broad range of functions and the knowledge and skill needed to do those functions, we can ask where and how it is possible to obtain them. We need not confine our search to the obvious: professional schools, apprenticeships, on-the-job training, experience, etc. The very technology with which we deal every day offers us many opportunities for innovation.

We should also not restrict our thinking to the practice of the professions as they are presently constituted, nor to their technology; we ought to concern ourselves with the theoretical base of both the profession and its technology.

Further, it can be very useful to look to many disciplines and professions, not just those whose relation to information work is obvious. Every discipline is potentially a contributor to IS, as well as a potential beneficiary. The involvement of the arts and humanities ought to be as great as of the sciences. We may strengthen the theory base of IS by infusions from those basic disciplines.

Mapping Relations

We need to map the relationships among the kinds of knowledge and skill required by the respective specialties within the information profession. Which elements do they have in common? Which occupations are most closely related, with respect to their educational needs, and would therefore be good candidates for inclusion in shared programs? What are the limits to such sharing?

It would be presumptuous of us to recommend realignments of professional organizations and of professional schools; such realignments are already happening, and we should look at them, asking their authors why they chose the options they did, and how those options are working out. We may explore how to encourage interaction among the professional societies and among the schools, and how they may develop a greater collegiality.

A Map of the Discipline

In the twenty year history of information science, many attempts have been made to draw a conceptual map of the discipline. Each of us attending the conference will have his or her own map, drawn out to a degree of detail dependent on how much we have thought about the matter.

We represent at least the three occupational groups identified, and the three contexts identified earlier, i.e., the professions, the disciplines, and the schools. There will surely be those among us whose customary point of view is turf, others whose outlook is more abstract, and still others who take a functional, pragmatic approach. However, none of us, I trust, is stuck in just one point of view; each will shift from one context and viewpoint to another throughout the meetings.

At the risk of being obvious, I suggest that we can help avoid confusion and dead ends if we remind ourselves from time to time which context we are addressing, and from which point of view.

I can think of several motivations for frank and friendly exchange of ideas among the members of this diverse group. There is a potential for helping us understand our own positions, and for planning, even if we end up, as we probably shall, planning different or even conflicting things. We can at least avoid wasteful duplication of effort if we know what one another is up to.

Finally, there is, I think, more to gain than to lose. We can gain valuable understanding from one another, while there is little prospect of our gaining or losing turf or prestige for our respective camps. In fact, the future probably will not belong to any of our professions, disciplines or schools. More likely the healthiest initiatives will come from people working in and with groups that claim only their partial and sometimes conflicting loyalties. In short, in their forum, we can afford to be both frank and friendly; we can ill afford not to be so.

REFERENCES

Borko, Harold. "Information Science—What Is It?". *American Documentation,* 19(1):3-5, January 1968.

Georgia Institute of Technology. *Proceedings of the Conferences on Training Science Information Specialists.* Atlanta: Georgia Institute of Technology, 1962.

King Research, Inc. *New Directions in Library and Information Science Education Newsletter.* 6000 Executive Boulevard, Rockville, MD 20852 (1984).

Wellisch, Hans. "From Information Science to Informatics: a Terminological Investigation." *Journal of Librarianship* 4(3):157-187, July 1972.

West, Martha W. *Research and Information Science: What Where We've Been Says About Where We Are.* Occasional Paper 32. Halifax, NS: Dalhousie University Libraries and Dalhousie University School of Library Science, 1983.

Wright, H. Curtis. "The Wrong Way to Go." *Journal of the American Society for Information Science.* 30:67-76; March 1979.

PART IV

GROUP DISCUSSIONS

Allen B. Veaner, Philip N. James – Rapporteurs
Florence M. Mason – Commentator

DISCUSSION OF PAPERS

SESSION I: FOUNDATIONS AND CONCEPTS

It was pointed out that information professionals from all three streams (information library science, IRM, MIS) must focus on information itself—content, intended use, "packaging", delivery, etc.—instead of the technology or similar secondary aspect of information delivery. Information professionals must learn how to manage information which is not necessarily neatly packaged such as conversations and other verbal communications, informal notes, pictorial allegations, and grafiti. Many forms of "messy" information exist and often can be the most relevant information yet none of the current informations systems has good methods for handling "messy" information.

All participants acknowledged that information can be used in many different ways: to support a decision making process, to build a knowledge base, to entertain, amuse, or edify. It is also used for education, research, easthetic, political and economic purposes.

It was stated that although information has value, its actual value is based on current or artificial use. R. Mason added to this that it is difficult to assess the value of information when one cannot anticipate its future use.

There was general agreement that all information professionals must design information systems. But it was also recognized that the nature of the systems depends upon both the tradition and values of each stream. Regardless of the information professionals' tradition or stream, the challenge is to become more pro-active in working with their clients. They must become more knowledgeable about their clients' needs and desires, be able to effectively package and deliver correct and relevant information. Information professionals must assume a leadership role in assuring that their systems and services are cost-effective for the enterprise and are most effective in serving the highest priority needs of their clients. It was noted that the two directions—high service goals and cost-effectiveness—may conflict yet must be satisfied. Attention was drawn to the fact that each individual client must be an active, enthusiastic supporter of the information management department and that senior management must see the information service department being cost-effective.

The related issue of the active role which information professionals must take in order to gain this strategic support was discussed. The following points were made:

1. The information professionals must become knowledgeable about the business of the enterprise;
2. The information professionals must design the information architechure and systems which support the enterprise;
3. The information professionals as catalysts must trigger the implementation of significant strategic uses of the information resources and
4. The information professionals must document persuasively the effectiveness of each strategic implementation on the enterprise.

Special attention was again drawn to the importance of the packaging and delivery of information. While information can meet every other standard of effectiveness, if it is not packaged and disseminated so that the client can use it effectively, it will not achieve its intended purpose.

There was a discussion of the changing values a curriculum should instill in its graduates. Students from any educational program must also demonstrate:

1. An ability to be sensitive and effectively responsive to technological and societal change
2. A perception that the career path is the management of information for use by people, not the management of information technologies
3. An ability to help those who have the high technical skills for building the complex technology infrastructure which supports society's information architecture.

The academic environment was discussed. The following institutional elements upon which a successful professional degree program for information professionals rests were suggested:

1. How well its students are grounded in basic disciplines
2. How well the information program can avoid turf battles with neighboring disciplines
3. How well the faculty can perform within existing reward structures
4. How sensitive and responsive the program is to rapid changes in the marketplace for its products—and how successful its graduates are
5. How effectively the program can identify and pursue a valid strategic vision for its own future
6. How effectively the program can retain the best and shed the worst of its own traditions; and how accurately the program is able to assess the professional and disciplinary value of their neighboring disciplines.
7. How well it prepares its graduates to make effective use of the interaction between theory and practice
8. How well it identifies and applies the dynamism inherent in its models to shape its programs of education and research
9. How well it "sells" its program so that potential information professionals can intelligently choose the field rather than simply fall into it.

It was observed that the discipline base and research paradigms for each of the fields included in information science needs to be better understood and articulated; and the need for understanding commonalities and relationships among the fields have to be accepted.

SESSION II: INFORMATION ARENAS AND APPLICATIONS: EDUCATIONAL IMPLICATIONS

Ben Franckowiak, Robert Grover – Rapporteurs.
Elizabeth Eddison – Commentator

Attention was drawn to the question of "core" knowledge or basic science for the three streams of IRM, MIS, and library and information science. It was argued that the knowledge core is the same, for fields but that their training and education differs depending on specific situations. To focus the discussion, Gordon Davis proposed the following schema:

INFORMATION SCIENCE DISCIPLINE

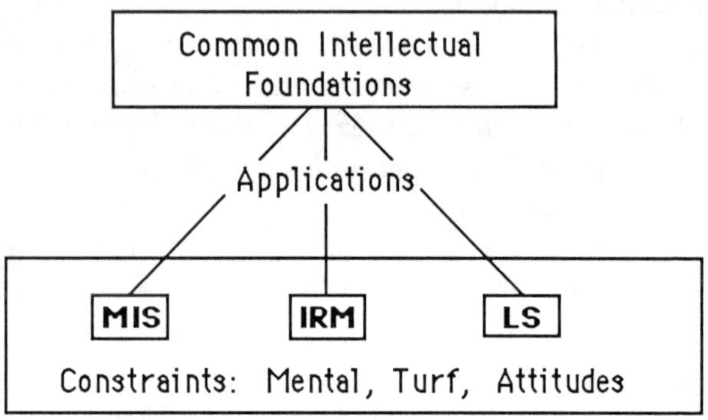

There was a general agreement with this model that the three streams draw from the same discipline and the difference arise in the exemplar—the applied fields. Some participants noted that while references have been made to a knowledge core common to information professions, the actual intellectual content of this core has not yet been discussed.

The discussion then focussed on the need to analyze and respond to market forces and the type of preparation necessary for the first professional job. A variety of issues were raised: the need to understand what information professionals are trained to do, the need to recognize that the programs are preparing entry level professionals, and the need to identify the job market and constant change within this market. There was also a general agreement on the need to teach about the change process—coping with and managing it.

It was stated that technology is a driving force because it allows for reduced cost and it enables us to expedite the movement of information. Technology has provided information professionals with unusual economic possibilities that naturally cause us to evaluate information management opportunities. It was felt that the proper application of technology will contribute towards achieving both business and humanistic goals.

It was asked to whom are we directing the graduates of new information education programs. The corporate market was mentioned earlier. It was pointed out that corporations do not have good information services and are not apprised of the competencies they need to expect from information managers. For example, those attending graduate programs in medicine, law, and business are not being educated as consumers and users of information. New MBA graduates are rarely trained in new information resources that are available to them and their enterprises. Corporations do not yet perceive the need for using information professionals and their tools and skills as part of their strategic vision.

Horton drew attention to the developments taking place in the federal government. The Paperwork Reduction Task Force recognized that information is not a free good but an organizational and manageable resource. The Task Force left the legacy of the 1980 Paperwork Reduction Act. Then, it was stated that the federal government wants academia to develop a curriculum for the education of information resource managers. It was pointed out that a graduate curriculum for IRM was established by the Department of Agriculture and neither library science, management information systems, nor information science was used as a model for the program. However, the curriculum at the Department of Agriculture is evolving. It was noted that it is still too early for this educational program to be frozen into a curriculum model.

The discussion shifted to how educational programs will implement concepts in educating people for information work. It was observed that in addressing the need for preparing information managers, library schools, for example, have added information science and information management courses with little definition of the fields. The following points were made:

1. Information professionals need to develop a philosophy of information use
2. They must be able to diagnose and anticipate the organization's information needs
3. They must be able to identify existing information in the enterprise
4. They must stimulate people to use information that is already available to them.

In designing an educational program for information managers, the question of the proper "role" for information professionals arose. It was argued that currently information professionals are chauffeurs or intermediaries, but what is needed are information pilots to assist executives in accessing information.

SESSION III: ASPIRATIONS FOR AN ACADEMIC DISCIPLINE

Fenwick F. Holmes – Commentator
Martha L. Hale – Rapporteur

Although this session originally was entitled "Aspirations for an Academic Discipline", it turned quickly into a discussion focusing on concepts of information. Holmes noted that throughout the conference session participants felt constrained by the barriers of not having a common language. We use like terms and attach different meaning to them. By doing so, we lose precision and, at the same time, foment misunderstanding. How are we to judge terminology used in the different fields represented at the conference? Holmes cited examples of terms that tended to separate our fields:

1. *Data* base can mean text in the library world and data in MIS
2. *Information science* is used in the library world to describe library studies; sometimes used in the MIS world as a synonym for information systems
3. *Information center* in the library world means to provide access to text data bases; in the MIS world, it means access to internal numeric data bases (e.g. how to use PC's and understand PC programs.)
4. *Information resource management* as interpreted in the federal government is different from the concept emerging in industry. Records management is not a synonym for either usage, but may be included in both.

Holmes mentioned that it was his opinion that this parallel process of like terms but different meanings was based on the fields' efforts to accommodate a common technological phenomena. This has led to semantic antagonism fueled by the lack of communication among the streams. The issue of "turf" as a problem, which repeatedly surfaced during the discussions is a manifestation of the unsettling convergence of technologies. The commentator suggested that since this convergence is a dynamic and on-going phenomenon, it would be a mistake to attempt too rigorous a definition of the boundaries of the three streams; we can't hide in our disciplinary bases any longer.

To illustrate his point of boundaries, Holmes suggested that Davis' view of MIS was broader than Swanson's. For example, Swanson considered the function of MIS to provide information for management decision-making through the exercise of Management Science and Decision Support systems. Davis, on the other hand, included in MIS the development of systems which have extensive human interface, such as accounting and expert systems. Holmes warned of the danger of abdicating the entire spectrum of application systems designed for users to computer science, which is more concerned with computer architecture, operating systems, compilers, and algorythms.

The commentator expressed reservation over McLean's MIS model cited in Davis' paper. This model indicates that the realm of MIS is that of the organizations information (presumably numeric) acquired internally through transaction-based systems. This information then forms corporate data bases serving the operational, tactical and strategic levels of management. Through the use of management systems/decision support systems and through these data bases, corporate decisions are made. He represented the situation as follows:

This relatively simple information pyramid was seen as "pre-Copernican". Not all corporate information is numeric and not all corporate systems are or will be mechanized. The model should also provide for the existence of corporate text:

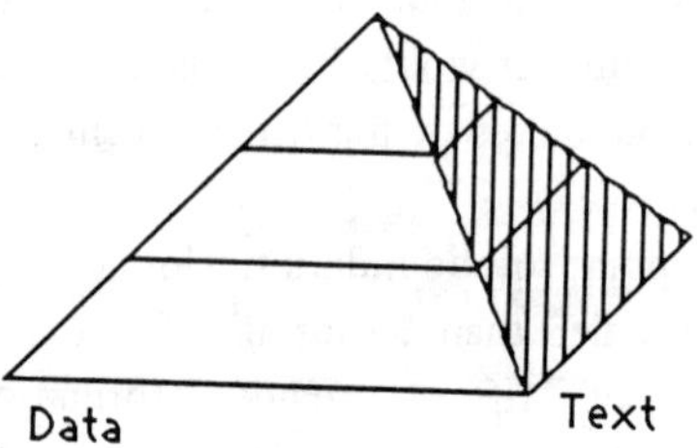

In addition, for decision-making, internal information simply is not sufficient and external numeric data bases can be used. Continuing (concatenation) external with internal numeric data bases allows for new understanding and value for decision making as seen below:

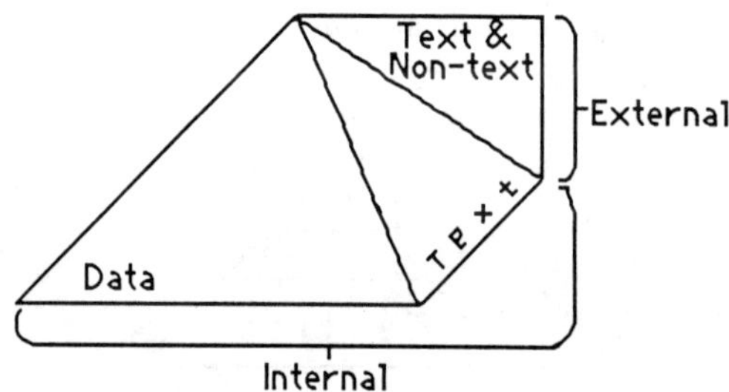

Finally, there is the world of external text and non-textual information that can be, and often is, drawn upon by executives in their decision making processes. The commentator suggested that the higher you go in the corporate ladder, the greater the need to access external, as opposed to internal information. This can be expressed as follows:

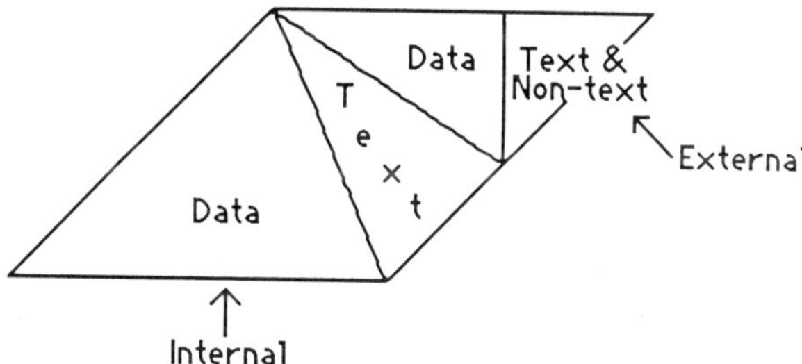

This model generated considerable discussion. It was pointed out that all levels of management within the enterprise have considerable need for external information. Some contributors to the discussion argued that the illustration is misleading if the external information pyramid is seen as indicating that the quantity of external information needed at the operational level is substantially less than the quantity of external information needed at the strategic level. However, there seemed to be an agreement that the information of the external world is essential to decision making.

Holmes also suggested and achieved general concurrence that organizations may have systems that are not computer-based, and that these are the legitimate domain of the MIS discipline. The commentator suggested that an important point in Donahue's paper was that the management of the records in MIS was not as important as creating new information which then had new value. This can be accomplished by finding and explaining new relationships between information from varied sources. Thus, information professionals should not eliminate the creation of new value from the information life cycle in the MIS or Information Science disciplines. Holmes also took issue with the "marking and parking" concept in the Buckland paper and suggested that there is a need to develop a more dynamic concept of information creation.

Holmes' comments directed the general discussion toward types of information used in enterprises. Two uses of the term "external information" emerged. External information is material created external to the organization and packaged in one of two ways—as databases or as written products. It appeared that the library science world referred to external information as written products created external to the organization. It was pointed out that supplying this type of information is the joining function of a corporate library. Such a library has added on-line data bases to its inventory but its traditional reliance on the printed word is a dominant part of its current image, or misimage. The second meaning of the term "external information" was verbal information, sometimes referred to as ephemeral information. Florence Mason pointed out that her recent study indicated that this type of information was the dominant type used by information managers. Swanson suggested that the intriguing part about this type of information is that it might be based on fact. Davis reported that the business school tradition is to teach people to be analytical; and, therefore, information systems people may not focus on how to deal with the variety of information being discussed even though there certainly is evidence that businessmen use each type of information described. He thought it would be more appropriate to use the terms of hard/soft data rather than external/internal information.

Florence Mason stated that information professionals need both the librarians' strategy to gather information and the information management strategy to repackage information into more usable formats.

Horton observed that there are now more than 5000 online databases, and from the information resource management perspective in the federal government, he expressed surprise that there had not been more emphasis on information in this format at the conference. It was generally agreed that the use of external data bases would continue to increase, but Swanson did not think that Chief Executive Officers spent or would spend much time with this type of external information.

Another variation on the discussion of types of information was presented by Eddison. She suggested that external information can be thought of in two ways: 1) as that which cannot be located within the organization and 2) as that which is externally generated. Holmes pointed out that internal information is not of purer grade than external information. He also suggested that there is a need for quality control in all types of information.

The area of information utilization was briefly discussed. It was pointed out that proximity or access may be deciding factors in the utilization of information. A reference was made to Buckland's earlier observations of people not even looking at information because they cannot get at it.

Then Davis listed areas where he thought conceptual "differences" existed among the three streams by listing concepts that were uniquely important to information systems. The divergences were:

1. Organization environments
   —organizational sciology
   —organization structure
   —organization functions and design
   —management and strategy
   —planning and control
2. Decision-making in an organizational context
3. Humans as information processes
4. Systems life cycles and large scale

These two lists generated untellectual debate among the group. (Unfotunately this text can only convey the ideas but not the intensity, excitement, and spirit that was generated by this listing of commonalities and differences among the streams). The library science stream took exception to Davis' divergency list and argued that these areas are also needed in their field.

Hale next focused the discussion on the question of theory and practice in the professions. She stated that rather than perceiving a dichotomy between practice and theory, one should analyze the concept on a continuum of levels of abstraction. Each level has a type of information which is appropriate and meaninfgul to those whose position requires that degree of abstraction. To illustrate her argument, Hale offered the following examples:

* practice-practice level of abstraction uses
  recipe information for concrete, shop level activities
* practice-theory level of abstraction uses
  middle range theories as information for organizational level
  activities
* theory-practice level of abstraction uses
  systems theory as information for interorganizational
  activities
* theory-theory levels of abstraction uses
  grand theory as information for societal level activities

What the group discovered in their discussions over what concepts were held in common and which were unique was that at the theoretical levels of abstraction of the concepts in both of Davis' lists there was commonality. However, at the other end of the continuum, at the practice level, when they described actual activities derived from those concepts, they differed.

Zachman shifted the discussion to the problems of finding a means for the group to develop a conceptual model for the information professions. He presented a "real world" model of the information professions drawn from a data processing perspective. He noted that this worldview as well as any other worldview may carry a predictable bias in its representation.

Starting the illustration of his viewpoint with computers, he stated that computers manage data which is arranged in "records" enabling the computer to manage it. A computer record is a "linear" representation of some facts (likely better referred to as "data," a term which does not connote value judgment about verity, validity, etc.). An example of a computer record is as follows: Employee No./Name/Address/etc. . . . Traditionally, such records are descriptive of the entities of a business or enterprise. In their aggregate, they describe the enterprise and as such they fall within the purview of a classic "Information Systems" part of the organization. The purpose of describing the enterprise with these records is to identify state or change of state so that appropriate action can be taken with regard to either the operation of the enterprise, or to improving the operation of the enterprise.

Attention was drawn to the technical challenge in managing these records and to define the relationships between all the records—that is, to define the "algorithm" that ties the records together, To monitor the accuracy or validity of the description of the record in order to precipitate appropriate actions, the relationship must be understood and managed. This is a complex engineering design problem.

Zachman pointed out that computers manage another kind of record, namely one that contains text, for example, line no./the/quick/brown/ fox. . . . The text is descriptive of ideas and often comes packaged in books or volumes. As such, the computers managing these kinds of records would normally fall within the purview of a library. The purpose of these kinds of records is to capture ideas not describe the enterprise.

This second type of record constitutes a body of knowledge which is vital to maintain if that body of knowledge is to be expanded. The emerging challenge here, of course, is to store huge volumes of text (records) and perform contextual searches and/or comparisons.

It was pointed out that computers also manage a third kind of record, one that contains a combination of "data" and "text." For example: Document 1/sender/receiver/data/the/quick/brown. . . . These records are descriptive of documents. The purpose of describing documents is to capture a "statement" for legal and/or historical purposes. These documents normally would fall within the domain of records management or archives. The challenge is to transmit the document from a sender to a receiver without losing it, and to "file" it in such a way that it can be retrieved should there arise a legal or historical reason to produce the record.

All three of the above described uses of computers can be found in a given organization or enterprise. This could be any enterprise. For example, a library needs to describe the enterprise (i.e. the library); to describe the ideas (e.g. books); and to describe the documents (e.g. abstracts, card catalog, etc.). Some contributors to this discussion observed that not all of the records that describe the enterprise may be automated; and not all documents nor all recorded ideas in the enterprise may be automated and managed by computers. It was noted by the group that the level of abstraction is one factor that is complicating our communication in the three streams of information professionals.

There was a general agreement that the human user and all the implications of the psychological and sociological impact of information are not represented in the model at this point. All that has been depicted is the representation of the information. The user is an additional dimension.

It was also agreed that the concepts discussed provide a conceptual model upon which to overlay the Greer topological model, and it also depicts the probable similarities and differences in the professional streams.

The following observations were made: When the profession deals with the representations, it is likely perceived as a manager of representations, the traditional role model. If the profession begins to deal with the context as well as the representation, then the profession likely becomes the content. Therefore, the information system becomes the business;

records/archives becomes the law/history; and the library becomes the body of knowledge.

The concluding thoughts were:

1. There is likely to be an underlying theory(-ies) orderly representing the information profession.
2. The Greer model would likely categorize and organize information about the theories.
3. Similarities and differences among the streams can be specified and described.
4. A core curriculum could likely be designed.

Group B: The relationship between an academic discipline and professional practice

Moderator: Michael K. Buckland
Rapporteur: Elizabeth Bole Eddison

The group was large (28 people) and disparate in focus. (Three-quarters of the group come from universities, but not all from universities with library or information science schools; the balance of the group was from a mixture of non-academic positions). The group had no representatives of the information resource management or records management points of view. There was one representative from Information Systems.

A number of points were made; each of which reflected the understanding of at least several people in the group, but at no time did the group endeavor to come to formal agreement or to arrive at a formal recommendation. The group concluded the following:

1. The relationship between an academic discipline and professional practice is inextricable. A discipline was identified as being fundamental, driven by curiosity; and professional practice is the application driven by the need to do something better. The motivations therefore are different. Each needs the other, but it is important at all times to keep the distinctions clearly in mind.
2. The Master's degree for information professionals could have a common core with different avenues of application leading from

the core. There was no focussed discussion as to what belongs in the core.

3. The Ph.D. is not a degree that is amenable to a sharing among disciplines, particularly since a doctoral program is to advance or expanded knowledge in a field through research.

4. There was concern about an undergraduate major in information science. It was felt that the distinction between the Bachelor's and the Master's programs would be unclear to employers. Development of analytical skills is important for information professionals. It was though that undergraduates lack sufficient experience to bring understanding and therefore analysis to pre-professional training.

5. Employers need to know what information professionals can do for them. The profession needs to educate the marketplace and the academic training at the master's level needs to produce graduates with useful skills, high standards, and an understanding of the profession's role in society.

Group C: What are the implications for the public/private sector?

—What is the place for a Chief Information Officer in a large enterprise?

—What would be an integrated executive program for Chief Executive Officers?

Moderator: Richard O. Mason
Rapporteur: Fenwick F. Holmes

This discussion session focused on the role of the Chief Information Officer (CIO) and the implications of this concept for the educational world. It was decided that since the CIO is an emerging phenomenon, the group needed to first examine the Information Resources Manager function and then determine what its relevance to the CIO might be. This logic was followed with considerable success.

The role of the IRM is prescribed in the public law known as the Paperwork Reduction Act. This law requires that there be established, in all agencies of the federal government, an Information Resource Management position to report to the head of the agency. This officer will be charged with planning, managing and controlling the information resource tools (e.g., communications, computers, word processing, personal computing, etc.) as well as the information assets (data and text). Although this officer may not have operating management control (tools and assets may be in departments not directly reporting to her), the planning and control responsibility are not diluted by the possibility of a dotted line relationship.

It was reported that several states are following the federal government concept of IRM. For example, South Carolina is establishing senior IRM positions which report to the heads of agencies and departments. Also at a state level an IRM position has been established and filled. This officer must interact with agency heads, the governor's office, and the legislature.

It was agreed that in analyzing state and federal examples, the IRM is not just a concept, but a specific family of jobs which has the force of law behind it and can therefore, specify its scope and areas of responsibility. At the federal level, over 5,000 such jobs already exist (although, in some instances, the title may be an additional duty of an official that was already in place (e.g. an undersecretary).

In both state and federal venues, these new posts represent not just single jobs, but a cluster of related positions to support the IRM function. This has significance in any examination of the potential market for IRM-related students.

The IRM position is not just a new name—it is a new job with more comprehensive responsibilities than those of the old MIS director or records manager. In South Carolina, for example, these jobs have been classified three job grades higher than the old MIS-type position.

It was pointed out, though, that while this process has already produced some 5,000 IRM jobs in the federal establishment, the concepts and positions are still evolving. The federal establishment is examining, via a Congressional committee, whether the spirit of the Paperwork Reduction Act has been carried out. In South Carolina, it was stated that IRM is an emerging concept, a "mosaic" which may not be representational of reality for another ten years.

There was little doubt in the minds of the conferees that the IRM concept represents a significant and persistent trend, that it involves a panoply of job opportuntiies in the public sector, and that the educational world has not addressed the training needs implicit in this trend. Horton suggested, both in the break-out session and in his paper, that the educational requirements in the federal government are being met through a USDA series of courses in the absense of suitable courses from academia.

Although there was less specific testimony about the adoption of the IRM concept in the private sector, it was the consensus of the group that the Chief Information Officer within the private sector would evolve into a counterpart of the public sector model. It was also suggested that at this stage in the evolution of the CIO concept, there is less recognition of the value of text as an information resource than there is in the IRM model. However, there is an increasing recognition of the need of external as well as internal information. Some industries information centers already make on-line text searching part of an information center function.

From this they concluded that the evolution of the CIO concept is toward the IRM arena and that the CIO, when the position emerges, will have the full range of attributes of the IRM executive: reporting to the highest level, concern with text as well as data, with internal as well as external sources, and full operating responsibility for the tools as well as the content side of information.

It was agreed that as the CIO function emerges, there will continue to be uneven and unequal development in different companies and industries. Before becoming an equal member of the partnership of CEO and COO, the CIO must "earn the spurs" and demonstrate an executive level comprehension of the enterprise's goals and the contribution of information to profit. Until that happens, the department will continue to be regarded askance as contributors to general overhead expense.

This then led the group to consider potential in these information-based jobs. The group saw several indications of real opportunity:

* The information industry is already made up of hundreds of companies generating billions of dollars in annual revenues with an overall growth rate of 28 1/2% per year.
* Information support roles within industry are increasing as the recognition of the value of information to achieve a competitive edge increases.

* The IRM and CIO concepts, previously discussed, point to an opportunity not yet adequately addressed by the academic world.

It was agreed that the converging streams of technology and information application have caused a blurring of boundaries among the traditional streams. This blurring also affects traditional functional boundaries between functions in industry. This, in turn, has resulted in a need to centralize control over the management of the tools of the information age in order to avoid exotic and uncontrolled proliferation of hardware and the development of redundant networks.

This convergence and blurring of boundaries makes it difficult to prescribe an ideal academic home for training and research on information age issues and practice. However, this difficulty should not deter academia and the other stakeholders from coming to grips with the issue now. While there is some degree of risk in presenting such guidelines for a curriculum at this time, the conferees felt that certain broad criteria should be kept in mind:

* Training for practitioners should involve MBA-type training.
* Accepted applicants should be of very high quality so that they can honestly aspire to the critically needed senior positions in government and industry.
* Applicants should be led to expect that they will start in industry in entry-level positions and earn their way to management through experience and demonstrated ability to put their academic education into practice.
* The value system of the library discipline should be a component of this training. The library world includes a strong service orientation and a commitment to ensure thorough feedback that the information provided gets the proper results.

While there is some degree of risk in presenting such a curriculum at this time, additional issues were discussed:

* Although IRM has become a mandated part of public sector job realities, the Civil Service Commission has not yet published an occupational series for these jobs. Furthermore, the Department of Labor has not updated its Dictionary of Occupational Titles to include the new family of jobs. There is no absolute assurance

that these lacunae will be filled before the first graduates of an "ideal" curriculum have graduated.
* Radical revision of curricula always risk problems with accreditation authorities as the process of accreditation often involves adherence to established norms; being innovative is not without risks.

Finally, the discussion led to a general structure for an MBA-type curriculum for Information Age Practitioners: It should be noted that any curriculum must be open-ended in view of the rapidity of change in technology and the explosion of research. Further, the reader should recognize that the list of included topics is very general and is intended to give only the essential flavor of each subject area:

I. *Organization and Management of Knowledge.* Included topics: Information Theory, Indexing, Abstracting, Cataloging, Service Systems Analysis, etc.
II. *Quantitative and Analytical Methods.* Included topics: Measurement, Economics, Operations Research/Management Science, Systems Development, Statistics, Cost/Benefit Analysis, etc.
III. *Communication.* Included topics: Written Communication, Oral Skills, Reading, Interviewing, Presentation Skills, Graphic Design, etc.
IV. *Management.* Included topics: Human Resources, Organizational Analysis, Management Systems, The Management of Information, etc.
V. *Technology.* Included topics: Data Bases, Personal Computing, Communications, Word Processing, and other Information Resource tools, etc.
VI. *Experiential.* It was felt that some form of internship of other experimental requirement should be a vital component of the curriculum.

The panel felt that because the field is constantly changing, there should be some provision for a continuing education requirement in connection with a Masters Degree. Whether this should take the form of continuing education in connection with a certification exam or a periodic return to academia, such as in renewing teaching credentials, was not discussed for lack of time. However, the panel felt that there was a need for a life-long education experience.

As a final thought, the panel noted that, whether a Master Degree level program such as this is or is not adopted, there will be a continuing need to:

* Put more business school know-how into our library schools, and
* Put more library school know-how into our business schools.

SUMMARY OF GROUP DISCUSSION REPORTS

Group A

The discussion focused on defining the boundaries of the three streams. Several models were examined as a basis for developing an outline of common concepts. A convergence and divergence list for the three streams was debated. Also discussed was the concept of levels of abstraction as a means of understanding commonalities. Attention was given to a "real world" model from data processing as a means of exploring the various conceptual models for the information professions. It was agreed that information professions need an underlying paradigm which could guide the design of a core curriculum.

Group B

The discussion ranged over a variety of topics: that there is an inextricable relationship between an academic discipline and professional practice, that Master's degree programs would have a common intellectual core, and that the Ph.D. degree is not shareable among disciplines. Attention was given to an undergraduate information science major and to marketing information professionals' utility. No formal consensus was achieved by the group.

Group C

The discussion concentrated on the nature of the Chief Information Officer. There seemed to be a consensus that the Chief Information Officer, within the private sector, will evolve as the counterpart to the Information Resource Manager of the public sector. It was pointed out that the IRM and CIO concepts had not been seriously addressed by the academic world. It was agreed that a blurring of traditional functional boundaries between traditional disciplines has taken place, stimulating the convergence of technology and information application. Attention was drawn to the type of education, values, and curricula that are needed. Examples of subjects and topics were listed. Finally, arguments were put forward for the importance of continuing education requirements.

GENERAL DISCUSSION

Group A had taken the position that the concept of a document life cycle model such as Donahue's represented a basic set of processes which could be seen as a foundation for the three fields represented at this conference. Several participants, however, pointed out the incompleteness of the model though it had been intended as a reasonable representation of the library tradition only where created documents are acquired. It was argued, for example, that even for the library and archival traditions, the cylce must end with a winnowing-out process which preserves the significant and destroys the trivial—where this distinction can be made for future use with confidence. This concept appears as "disposition" at the end of the revised model. Mason suggested that Donahue's model is too neat and, unfortunately, avoided a myriad of necessary but messy activities like fixing, suppressing, and reintegrating.

Discussion focussed on the "create" end of the model which to some suggested an area thus far omitted from the discussions. An argument was put forward that information originates from every discipline, and many other disciplines, like those at the conference, deal with information about information; examples of journalism and economics were mentioned.

Comments were made regarding the role of the arts in the representation and delivery of information. All the arts, the graphic, fine, and performing arts are involved in the information transfer process. The television commercial was cited as an excellent example of the persuasive packaging and delivery of information. Arguments were put forward for the need to examine the effective management of information resources in all forms of representation.

In response to Group B's report the discussion concentrated on the role of the Ph.D. degree. D'Elia pointed out that the purpose of doctoral studies has been to build a knowledge base and that undergraduate studies draw from this creation of knowledge. At the master's level educators tend to draw ideas from the broader range of disciplines and professions to prepare students to enter the professions. Another view for shaping a professional Ph.D. program is to design a program so that the doctoral faculty's teaching is more strongly influenced by the practitioners rather than by the discipline's research. It was pointed out that this would mean that the Ph.D. becomes an extension of the Master's Degree. If this becomes a model, then undergraduate degrees in information science merely represent a watered down master's degree program rather than being built on the research of the discipline.

Orgren commented that the role of the university is in conflict: there are those who believe it exits to create new knowledge and to disseminate this knowledge, and there are those who, because of the declining market for their graduates, wish to follow market demands. Professional schools are caught between the academic vision of the university vice president and the market needs of professional practice. The professional school's legitimacy in academia is questioned by the vice president who is committed to knowledge creation and the intellectual components of education. Some participants suggested that this tension between the demands of education and the marketplace might be creative rather than destructive.

Also discussed was whether a common core curriculum could address the three streams adequately even if the disciplinary bases were the same. No clear conclusions were reached, but Greer pointed out that since everything we do in information management with the three streams is driven by people for whom we design information delivery systems, the core program must help students understand and deal effectively with people and their uses of information.

The discussion then turned to the characteristics of various existing education programs. Swanson reported that UCLA's MBA program demands demonstrated quantitative skills and some full-time experience in the world of work from entering students. Students there can package their educational programs to meet their specific needs. UCLA's MBA and Ph.D. are two distinct pathways; the MBA is not a milestone enroute to a Ph.D.

Mason explained that the University of Arizona undergraduate MIS program is heavily weighted toward the disciplines associated with creating a computer-based information system and with the management of a department which creates such systems. Mason also observed that this educational program is broadening to include decision support systems, end-user computing, and strategic use of the internal machine-readable information resource, and associated telecommunications capabilities. However, there is little or no exposure to library science, records management, or any of the current derivations of these traditions.

The following issues were raised briefly: (a) universities' need to "follow the market" and the field's attempt to preserve the values associated with the knowledge area which has a declining market; (b) a field of knowledge's need to continually assess and redefine itself in relation to the real world; (c) yielding to the homogenizing effects of the accreditation processes; and (d) the field's need for creating new knowledge and disseminating it to the field through the entry of new professionals.

The discussion turned to the employers who appreciate our educational products. It was suggested that employers do not generally appreciate the long-term value of employees and too often seek out those with the entry level specific skills at the lowest price. For example, CPA firms seek cheap accountants, architectural firms seek cheap draft persons, etc. The tendency is to select the best performers from among existing employees for promotion rather than hiring better prepared masters level people. This is particularly true when a field is growing rapidly. There was agreement that a person with a broad liberal arts undergraduate background and a professional master's degree is a better long-term bet for an employer than a person with a professional baccalaureate. However, employers—even those who pay lip service to this premise—have a tendency to overlook it in hiring.

Generally, there seemed to be no support at the conference for a professional undergraduate "information degree." An "information" major imbedded in a strong liberal arts program followed by a professional master's degree seemed to be the preference, despite the contrary behavior of the marketplace. At the professional master's level, there is a felt responsibility to prepare graduates for a lifelong career which may include several changes of fields.

Also discussed were the role and purpose of the accreditation process. Divergent views of accreditation were expressed. On the one hand accreditation was seen as the keeper of traditional values and highly resistant to innovation. On the other, there were those who felt that accreditation bodies were receptive to innovations which were well conceptualized and rooted in a sound intellectual base. Perhaps this reflects differences in approaches among the accrediting bodies themselves.

It was underlined that many of the model's developed during the preparation for this conference, and also conceptualized in debate, can form a basis for rigorous, disciplined-based research and as the base for articulating the intellectual foundations of the emerging information science discipline. These models should be seen as dynamic and not static representations of a research agenda for the discipline of information science. They should always be subject to change in light of research findings from other disciplines and practical application from employers.

It was observed that the MBA professional degree is rooted in well-defined academic disciplines like economics, psychology, mathematics, etc. The same disciplinary bases does not exist for the MLS. Arguments were forwarded that the MLS curriculum needs to acquire its intellectual base and its market direction concurrently in order to develop leadership for the future; the marketplace has a way of rewarding the institutions it feels can respond to its needs. It was thought that a whole spectrum of programs may be needed, not simply a professional master's or a more rigorous doctorate. It was said that the whole spectrum of program needs must be discussed together as a unit. It is that "whole spectrum" of what constitutes the discipline of information science that needs careful exploration.

Herbert K. Achleitner and
Martha M. Hale

AFTERWORD
In Search of Conceptual Harmony

Perhaps it is useful at this point to briefly reflect on the ideas discussed at this conference. While this conference clearly did not attempt to develop a grand map, signposts for the information science discipline were desired. To achieve this goal, the participants were asked to analyze the commonalities and differences of the three intellectual streams, to identify the shared or exclusive subject areas within the pool of knowledge and to discuss appropriate criteria for the education of information professionals.

The purpose of this final chapter is to describe the dynamics of the conference—the sociology of knowledge creation—and to provide the reader with a framework for understanding the report of the generation discussion, group meetings, and plenary sessins which are found in the preceding chapter, one about the process of conferencing, another about the content of the discussions.

The sponsors of the conference saw the process of conferencing as a means of information creation and dissemination, which it clearly proved to be. It had been assumed that a conference environment—its purpose, papers, discussion, and interaction—would permit people to process and refine the thoughts presented by the speakers. This book is an attempt of the commentators, rapporteurs, and editor to introduce the reader of the ideas that the conference participants began building.

Patterns of listening and responding were slow in developing, perhaps because participants' roles determined how they processed information. Each category of participants, educators, consultants, and practitioners had a different perspective of their profession because of their roles. These roles appeared to be more influential than the apparent historical separation of the three streams—librarianship, information systems, and information resource management, including archives and records management—which the participants represented.

The ideas of the conferees were shaped by their association with their world. John von Maan's observation "Where I stand depends on where I sit,"* seems to be particularly appropriate in explaining the dynamics of the first two days of the conference. Comments tended to take the form of mini-speeches, staking out turf, rather than responding to another's ideas and communicating with each other during the sessions. Participants evidently needed time to listen to each other, to understand a given speaker's conceptual framework as well as the language and meaning employed. Because of mixing the roles and streams, mixing of historic traditions, values, ideologies, research paradigms, and social purpose, the conference's goals were more slowly realized than we had hoped. Hindsight shows us that the conference format did not encourage a focus on the ideas presented in the papers. By no means, however, should these observations be construed as negative criticisms but simply a recording of events.

It was not until the discussion following Session III that the participants began to respond to each other directly. They began to see their own streams through the eyes of others. Librarians, for example, had not known that the other streams appreciated their service orientation. Two educators, one from information system and one from library science, discovered that they were both involved in user behavior research using quantitative methods. Once such interpersonal communications had paved the way, the participants were more willing to address each others ideas.

In order for the reader to understand the proceedings recorded in this book, it is now important to highlight some of the issues addressed or ignored. The juxtaposition of discipline and practice had been a key issue in developing the conference theme and in posing the discussion questions for the group sessions. In his paper, Davis responded to this by distinguishing an academic discipline from the so-called applied fields whose educational packages are derived from what is going on in current practice. His criteria for a discipline were: 1) long-term orientation, 2) course content based on underlying principles and concepts of the field,

---

* Van Maanen, John. The Fact and Fiction of Organizational Ethnography. *Administrative Science Quarterly*. Vol. 24, No. 4 (December 1979: 539-50.

3) formulation of new answers as the field changes, 4) and faculty are evaluated on their command of underlying principles, concepts, and phenomena as expressed by research and publications. He stated:

> Both the vocational and the academic discipline approachs are valuable and have their place in our educational system. However, within the context of the university, a field will never flourish unless it is an academic discipline.

Also discussed was the drive for academic respectability, a common need of all new disciplines. This respectability, whose accepted signposts are established research paradigms, is of particular interest in the three streams, for their survival is at stake. Each professional field seems to lack a portion of the educational package demanded in the academic tradition. Library science educators, for example, have been accused of lacking a sound theory base. Information resource management, according to Horton, is waiting for the development of appropriate curricula, while Warner observed that archivists lack a clear identity. Fugate noted that records management lacks the application of social science theories that can explain the creation, diffusion and utilization processes. Having thus acknowledged the need for a framework, the conference speakers offered several frameworks for the study of information.

Both Buckland and Donahue cast the study of information in a "representation of knowledge" context. Buckland observed that viewing information studies broadly, a variety of disciplines such as linguistics, cognitive science, cybernetics, and artificial intelligence are contributors to understanding information.

Swanson's framework of information study took a more specific view. His list for a foundational field includes: computer science, management sciences, organizational sciences, and for foundational elements were data, software, hardware, problems, models, solvers, individuals, organizations, and institutions.

Richard Mason's conceptual framework was based on economic consideration for designing an information system. He developed an information value and cost model which started from the societal perspective that information serves a purpose, and that information has actual and potential use. Mason then offered a theory of value that includes four categories:

economic, scientific, political, and aesthetic. He also included in his model
the notion of attributes, specifically relevance (wants, needs, availability),
clarity, timeliness, reliability, and validity.

Davis observed in his paper that "models and frameworks are useful in
defining research, specifying variables, and developing a research tradition."
He offered an information systems research model consisting of:

A. Environmental variables
   1. External environment
   2. Organizational environment
   3. User environment
   4. Information System developed environment
   5. Information System operations environment
B. The Information subsystem
   1. Content variable
   2. Presentation form variable
   3. Time of presentation variable
C. Process variables
   1. Development process
   2. Operations process
   3. Use process

Davis also focused on the importance of the relationship between subfields
in information systems and their reference disciplines, for example:

Subfield	*Reference Discipline*
Information systems organization	Organization and management
and management	Organization sociology
Examples:	Organization psychology
Information system planning	Organization behavior

Thus, Davis links information systems organization and management to
the underlying academic disciplines of sociology, psychology, organization and management.

Greer offered a similarly broad academic perspective for library and information science research. His model was based on the processes common
to all information professions.

1. Responsibility for the design and management of an information sys-
   system encompassing a database.
2. Responsibility for the design and management of an organization
   consisting of staff, equipment, space and financial resources to provide the interface between the information system and the potential
   user.
3. Responsibility for accommodating the information needs and behavioral characteristics of a specific client population.
4. Responsibility for the commodity "information" and the objective
   of enhancing the processes of information transfer.

If these processes are examined within the existing policy and environmental context using the relevant theories and research methodologies
they can be translated into a core theory base for a discipline of information science. A research model of these four fields (information engineering, information organization management, information psychology,
and sociology of information) can be presented as follows:

Figure 2

A research model for information science

With their focus on the theory base or reference disciplines, the Greer and
Davis models have taken the broadest perspectives of the underpinnings
for an information science discipline. Mason too, in his analysis of individual needs, the environment, organizational context, and mode of representation presented a broad picture of the discipline. Buckland's concern

with the creation and use of representations of knowledge argued also for similar needed key elements for an information science research model. Although they offered conceptual frameworks, they largely ignored the organizational issues that would affect the formation of an underlying discipline for the information profession.

It was also realized, but not discussed in depth, that the three streams were not equally powerful. Information resources management, records management, and archives management are applied fields developing from what is going on in practice. Therefore, their strength and format varies from location to location, and linkages were desirable in order to strengthen their connections with the private sector. An information systems program is part of a larger and currently powerful unit, the business school and business degree. Its students study in other departments but within the business school for their interdisciplinary linkages. Like the business school, the library science school is also an independent unit, but does not have interdisciplinary linkages within its own organizational unit. This may explain why the impetus for a conference that would facilitate cross-school linkages came from library science educators who have been fielding questions on their campuses abut their academic respectability.

Two other content issues that would affect any future design of an integrated educational program were largely ignored throughout the conference. Implicit throughout the conference was the suspicion that the role of the university vis-a-vis professional education should be debated. This debate of education versus training hung covertly over most of the conference. Not until the final session did this issue surface. The role of theory in the preparation of professionals, while explicitly stated in almost all papers, was treated as a step-sister during the discussions.

The last issue which was also basic to the conference theme largely remained unapproached: Should educators attempt to move toward a discipline? Greer's paper assumed the answer was yes; Swanson and Davis wrote that information systems had already done so. Perhaps the differences among the three contributors was in their definition of the breadth of a discipline and the nature of paradigms a discipline must have. It must also be noted that there was an underlying suspicion by some participants that intellectual foundations were an unnecessary discussion.

Having resolved neither the issue of an information science discipline's nature nor the issues of the role of a professional program's role in a university and among the disciplines, the conferees did, however, repeatedly discuss the concept of information in terms of four commonalities. First, information is a societal product (numeric, textual, structural, relevant, etc.) created in a particular environmental context. Second, the importance of information utilization has driven all streams to realize that the focus of an information system must be on potential users and, therefore, there is a need to examine human use of information. Next, information professionals work within an organization devoted to the delivery of information products; and the management of that organization must be considered a part of any educational program. Finally, all information programs must prepare professionals to create, adopt and utilize the technology that will most efficiently and effectively bring the product to the people. The roots of a discipline can be found in these commonalities.

The theme of common intellectual foundations for research and curriculum development was what attracted most people to this conference. Their need to begin coming to terms with our twentieth century obsession with information transfer was apparent. What was also apparent was that the building of a common paradigmatic vision is a process that cannot be easily accomplished by one conference. What divides the streams and roles —the history, values, professional tradition and levels of abstraction—is too ingrained to be easily overcome. But what was accomplished was that we introduced a dialogue among individuals within various fields and that we started the process of examining each other's research models and requirements. After all, what we really attempted to do, and must continue to do, is to create a megadiscipline such as history or anthropology which can then accommodate the many streams. To do that and thereby meet society's needs brings us closer to the question of "What is to be done."

CONTRIBUTORS

Speakers:

Michael Buckland
Assistant Vice-President of Library Plans and Policies
Office of the President
University of California, Berkeley

Gordon B. Davies
Honeywell Professor of Management Information Systems
School of Management
University of Minnesota

Joseph C. Donohue
College of Library and Information Science
University of South Carolina

Rena L. Fugate
President, Project Completers
Glendale, California

Roger C. Greer
Dean, School of Library and Information Management
University of Southern California

Forest Woody Horton, Jr.
Information Consultant
Washington D.C.

Richard O. Mason
MIS Department, School of Business and Public Administration
University of Arizona

E. Burton Swanson
Graduate School of Management
University of California, Los Angeles

Robert Warner
Archivist of the United States

Rapporteurs:
Ben Franckowiak
Dean, Graduate School of Librarianship and Information Management
University of Denver

Martha L. Hale
School of Library and Information Management
University of Southern California

Allen B. Veaner
Principal, Allen B. Veaner Associates
Toronto, Canada

Commentators:
W. Stanely Brown
Libraries and Information Systems Center
Bell Laboratories
Murray Hill, New Jersey

Elizabeth Eddison
President, Warner-Eddison Associates
Cambridge, Massachusetts

Fenwick Holmes
President, International Academy at Santa Barbara
Santa Barbara, California

Philip James
Director, Information Institute
International Academy at Santa Barbara
Santa Barbara, California

Donald Marchand
Director, Graduate School of Information Management
Technology and Policy
College of Business Administration
University of South Carolina

Florence M. Mason
Graduate Library School
University of Arizona

Jane Robbins-Carter
Director, Library School
University of Wisconsin, Madison

John Zachman
IBM
Los Angeles, California

Conference Chair:
Herbert K. Achleitner
School of Library and Information Management
Emporia State University
Emporia, Kansas

Co-Sponsor:
Eric H. Boehm
Chairman of the Board
International Academy at Santa Barbara
Santa Barbara, California